Forgotten Borough

Forgotten Borough

Writers Come to Terms with Queens

Edited by

NICOLE STEINBERG

excelsior editions

State University of New York Press
Albany, New York

Published by
State University of New York Press, Albany

For information, contact State University of New York Press, Albany, NY
www.sunypress.edu

Excelsior Editions is an imprint of State University of New York Press

Production by Ryan Morris
Marketing by Fran Keneston

Library of Congress Cataloging-in-Publication Data

Forgotten borough : writers come to terms with Queens / edited by
  Nicole Steinberg.
    p. cm.
  A collection of essays, travelogues, poems.
  ISBN 978-1-4384-3583-1 (hardcover : alk. paper)
  1. Queens (New York, N.Y.)—Literary collections.   2. City and town life—
New York (State)—New York—Literary collections.   3. American literature—
New York (State)—New York.   I. Steinberg, Nicole.

PS549.N5F67 2011
810.9'9747243—dc22   2010020728

10 9 8 7 6 5 4 3 2 1

In memory of my mother, Susan Steinberg,
the queen of Queens

Contents

Acknowledgments   ix

Introduction: Between the Boulevards   1
Nicole Steinberg

85-11 Avon Street   7
Julia Alvarez

To Bridge: The Spaces Between, Behind, and Around Us   13
Buzz Poole

Love and Shame   21
Margo Rabb

Waiting for Big Bird   25
Marcy Dermansky

Thinking on the N   31
Susan Y. Chi

Chuckie   39
Victor LaValle

Ethelerie's Blank Check   43
Arthur Nersesian

The Maspeth Holders   57
Margarita Shalina

Three Poems   71
Nicole Cooley

The Sunnyside Shuffle   75
  Ron Hogan

Eating East Elmhurst   81
  Molly McCloy

High Q   91
  Roger Sedarat

God Lived in Queens   99
  Jayanti Tamm

How to Disappear Completely   105
  John Weir

Snow Forts   117
  Robert Lasner

Four Poems   127
  Juanita Torrence-Thompson

A Queens Necropolis: The Burial and Building of New York   133
  Marc Landas

Rockaway Sonnets   147
  Jill Eisenstadt

Accent Reduction   151
  Mark Swartz

Koshchei the Deathless   157
  Irina Reyn

Neighborhood #3 (Power Out)   173
  Marissa Walsh

The Children   175
  Jocelyn Lieu

Flight   183
  Rigoberto González

Notes and Permissions   199

Contributors   201

Acknowledgments

My deepest thanks to all of the contributors for sharing their numerous gifts and talents.

I can't bestow enough gratitude upon Marissa Walsh, who supported the little book that could from its infancy and held my hand the entire way, answering late-night phone calls, responding thoughtfully to aggravated e-mails, and shelling out for margaritas at happy hour when necessary. This book would not exist without her guidance, friendship, and encouragement.

In addition, thank you to the following kind souls who offered love and sensitive ears along the way: Susan and Louis Steinberg, Jessica Diebold, Danny Foceri, Molly McCloy, Rebecca Curtiss, Amanda Wilson, Mary Poole, Elisabeth Bayer, Peter Bogart Johnson, Michael J. Andrews, Eleanor Russell, Alexis Boehmler.

And thank you to Queens for raising me, letting me go, and staying put until I return.

Introduction:
Between the Boulevards

Nicole Steinberg

Imagine having to take the 7 train to the ballpark, looking like
you're [riding through] Beirut next to some kid with purple hair
next to some queer with AIDS right next to some dude who just
got out of jail for the fourth time right next to some 20-year-old
mom with four kids. It's depressing.

—John Rocker, former Major League Baseball relief pitcher

It's not the prettiest borough; upon first glance, not the most memorable.
Some parts are nice to look at, if suburbia puts you at ease or if you enjoy
the passing view of graffiti-adorned Five Points, from the window of an
aboveground 7 train. It's rare that you'll hear people wax poetic about
Queens the way they might over the concrete canyons of Manhattan or
the beauteous brownstones of Brooklyn. The Bronx enjoys a reputation
for grit and authenticity, and even Staten Island retains a place in many
a New Yorker's heart as the mysterious underdog, a place people love to
hate even if they've never been there. People tend to forget about Queens.
They're surprised to hear that culture exists here, too, as if some kind of
force field exists along the righthand side of the East River. When the
Museum of Modern Art moved part of its collection to Long Island City
in 2002, art lovers lauded the results; now the MoMA QNS building,
once a Swingline staple factory, stands as a big, blue, abandoned carcass—a
testament to New York's short-term memory. For the recent city transplant,

1

Queens is often a footnote, a destination that makes a rare appearance in the New York index, only on those days when Indian food sounds good or there's an afternoon Mets game to attend. Me? I'm in love with Queens, my home borough and final destination, wherever I may travel. While others neglect its presence in favor of supposedly more exciting places, I'm constantly pulled back by the force of its magnetism—the wealth of culture, diversity, and history that translates into possibility. I'm a Queens girl, through and through, with my long fingernails and hoop earrings, my love of animal prints and propensity to wear too much eyeliner. I've suffered the sting of backhanded compliments such as, "She's such a Queens girl, yet she's highly educated," and I've put up with friends who never dared to tread across the Queensboro Bridge. Still, nothing can tarnish my Queens pride, passed down from my mother to the kid who always sat in the passenger seat beside her, watching the sights fly by: the Russian storefronts of Rego Park, the bodegas of Corona, Rockaway's boardwalks, the World's Fair Unisphere in Flushing Meadow Park, innumerable historic cemeteries, and the open roads of expressways and highways, stacked and winding and stretched for miles.

I grew up between boulevards, in a co-op by the intersection of Junction and Northern Boulevards. My grandparents left the Bronx and transplanted the Rosenberg family to this very building when my mother was fourteen years old. Junction serves as the borderline between two distinctly different neighborhoods: to the east, ethnically diverse Corona, filled with housing projects and overlooking the relics of the 1964–65 World's Fair, as well as the Queens Museum of Art and CitiField, risen from the ashes of Shea Stadium; to the west, historic Jackson Heights, where my mother attended school—a place I remember for its Tudor-style homes, the lush gardens of St. Mark's Episcopal Church, and rows of sturdy trees that lined the way home from preschool. My mother's walks home were never leisurely; I recall tales of bullies who chased her down Northern Boulevard, hollering nasty names, as if this place didn't belong to her—as if *she* didn't belong. Yet she was resilient enough to stay despite the inauspicious start, talented and sharp enough to become a leader in her field, educating thousands of Queens schoolchildren, and stubborn enough to raise a child of her own in Queens, taking the borough into her heart and carving out a home.

The Kent building, sandwiched between the Lawrence and the Jackson in the Southridge co-op complex between Northern and 34th Avenue, will always be my safe haven, home to two apartments that served as the backdrop of my childhood. My parents bought their co-op a year before I was born, soon after they married and my mother's surname went from

Rosenberg to Steinberg. We lived on the fifth floor in apartment 5V (*V as in Victor*, we always told delivery boys). My bedroom was stuffed with toys and hardly ever clean, much to my father's dismay; it overlooked the playground downstairs, where I slid down the slide, rode the seesaw, and avoided the threatening heights of the monkey bars.

Then there was my grandparents' third-floor home with its rich, chocolate-colored carpeting, library of encyclopedias, and a bedroom reserved for me that once belonged to my mother and aunt. I slept over often, usually after our weekly Wednesday night dinners. Marion, my grandmother, would make something delicious—potted chicken, meatballs and spaghetti, hamburgers—and my great aunt Elsie arrived with the same box of assorted cookies from the same Manhattan bakery she always frequented. We'd pretend to enjoy the rest of the cookies after we divvied up the precious tricolor marzipans. On weekends, during the spring and summer, I'd listen for the familiar jingle of the Mister Softee ice cream truck downstairs and drag my grandmother along, as if life itself depended on catching the truck before it fed all the neighborhood children, then departed—as if it wouldn't sit in that same spot all day, as it always did. I could see my grandparents' bedroom from my own and I always tried to catch my grandmother looking out her window, so we could wave and exchange a serendipitous smile.

Junction Boulevard didn't truly become a part of my daily life until later in my adolescence, when the rides home from school ceased and the bus and subway were the only viable options. The stretch of Junction between Northern Boulevard and Roosevelt Avenue has always been a sort of city unto itself, the dominant ethnicities constantly changing over time. As I grew older, I resented the boulevard for its distinct lack of gentrification while other streets in Jackson Heights got their Starbucks and FYEs. Though I could usually make the trek to the 7 train without anyone's notice, I did get the occasional catcall of "Yo, Vanilla," which left me feeling completely out of place in a moving cloud of Dominican, African American, and Korean neighbors. Still, I took advantage of what Junction had to offer: mainly a plethora of ninety-nine cent stores, two Payless Shoes locations, and beauty supply shops that offered designer hair products at half the usual price. There was also a Wendy's, which morphed into a KFC, then a Duane Reade pharmacy, and now stands as a decimated, empty lot after an unfortunate fire, waiting to be rebuilt into someone else's vision.

I returned to Junction after college, then left soon after I completed grad school, relocating to another infamous boulevard: Queens Boulevard, known as both a fertile breeding ground for cross-culture life, and as a death trap for hurried pedestrians, unwilling to wait for the light to change. My first apartment was on 40th Street in Sunnyside, a block away from the heavy traffic of the boulevard, smack-dab in an immigrant-heavy neighborhood that enjoyed the diversity of Russian grocery stores, Halal markets, British import shops, and too many Thai restaurants to count. In the summertime, I could grab fresh fruit on a Saturday morning from the nearby farmer's market and sit on a park bench, rows upon rows of postwar buildings to the south and Manhattan's gleaming skyline to the west. I was so close to Manhattan and yet everything I needed was right there in Sunnyside, easily within reach. A short trip on the Q60 bus route took me all the way down the boulevard to the Queens Center mall, a place my parents hated to visit in the '80s, cramped for space and filled with people who seemed to speak in every language except English. Now, the mall is three times as big, chock-full of high-end shops. In high school, my friend Hai-Phung and I would sometimes take a bus there after school, browse and eat in the food court; then we'd sit outside, whiling away the time and feeling rebellious, until she had to travel home to the Bronx and cook dinner for her Vietnamese family.

My mother saw to it that the most pervasive boulevard of my young life was Northern Boulevard, which stretches, long and lazy, all the way across the northern part of the borough, from Long Island City to Little Neck. Afraid that I wouldn't get the best education back in Jackson Heights or Corona, she pulled strings and enrolled me in elementary school in Bayside, an affluent neighborhood that many newcomers to New York have never seen nor visited. While we stayed put on Junction and Northern throughout my childhood, my first real friends all lived a half-hour away in Bayside, where my mother worked and longed to reside as well. They enjoyed suburban lifestyles in two- and three-story homes, content with their outdoor shopping centers and general lack of culture. Still, I sniffed out a hint of diversity in Bayside, a glimmer of the immigrant dream: While one friend's mother had never met a Jew before me, another friend's grandmother chopped the heads off chickens on the kitchen counter, Chinese soap operas on television providing constant background noise.

Because my mother worked at Bayside High School and I attended school nearby, we were constantly on the move between townships, the connecting road being Northern Boulevard. Name any place along its winding path and I'm sure to have a memory of it. I remember bus rides to Main Street, Queens' answer to Chinatown, where my friends and I frequented our favorite pizzeria and then went home for dinner as if nothing had happened; or the time my parents took me to see *Who Framed Roger Rabbit?* at the theater near Northern's intersection with Crocheron Avenue. The film scared me so much, I had nightmares for weeks; I'd turn my head away from the window whenever we passed the theater thereafter, until it shut down and made way for a Korean club.

Go farther east on Northern and you'll hit the intersection with Francis Lewis Boulevard, close to I.S. 25, where I attended middle school. Farther than that is the Bayside Diner, right off the Cross Island Expressway—a favorite eatery of my family's, reserved for special occasions when the Mark Twain Diner in Jackson Heights wouldn't cut it (which also happens to reside on Northern Boulevard and where my father still goes most mornings for English muffins with cream cheese). Though my mother and grandparents are no longer around, I like to go there with my father now and imagine my mother sitting at the table beside me, pulling the Melba toast from the bread bowl; Seymour, my grandfather, returning from the restroom, a slight wobble to his otherwise powerful stride, wondering aloud where the goddamn check is already.

Beyond Bayside, there is Alley Pond Park, then Douglaston and Little Neck—places that exist in my head almost as a dream, as I grow older and lose more of the people who share in my memories. Here, you'll find the Stop & Shop supermarket, which my grandparents frequented every week, despite the fact that it was forty-five minutes away, and their favorite MSG-free Chinese restaurant. And there are even more diners—the Seville (now closed), the Scobee, the Seven Seas—each of which my family derided for their own special reasons. In a way, I feel more connected to these neighborhoods than I do to Jackson Heights and Corona, which both existed right outside my door for years. Though we lived close to the city (code for Manhattan, for those not raised in Queens) and couldn't afford to leave, my mother made sure that I got the idyllic suburban childhood—that I never found myself fleeing from bullies and racing down the street, desperate to get home. Yet, at the time, I felt a different kind of loneliness: a feeling of never quite belonging anywhere I went. Though the color of my skin matched those of my elementary school classmates, it didn't stop the occasional rat-faced kid from spitting "Happy *Hanukkah*" at me in a mocking tone. And when I attended Jewish day camp during the summers, I was seen as the Other by Long Island princesses who had never stepped foot past Douglaston—a city girl from Queens, no better than trash, all because I lived on the wrong end of Northern Boulevard.

Looking back, I know I'm lucky. I'm not just from a particular area of Queens, but rather the entirety of it: the largest borough in New York and most diverse county in America, with two major airports, numerous roadways, and a long list of neighborhoods. Each street, each avenue, each corner belongs to me. The idea for this anthology came to me when I realized that most people don't know Queens the way I do, nor the way my mother did, and yet there are so many stories to tell. The borough's contributions to pop culture run the gamut from the Ramones to Ron Jeremy, LL Cool J to Fran Drescher; it's the final resting place of Louis Armstrong and the birthplace of hip-hop legend Run DMC, who once announced to the world, "*It's Christmastime in Hollis, Queens.*" In Queens, we do our best to triumph over class-related adversity and we share the unique aspects of our cultures; we grow up in the isolated shadow of old industry, yet we welcome visitors from all parts of the world; we pack the 7 train when the Mets hit a winning streak and we still root for them when they lose—and they lose a lot, but we love them anyway.

With so much of my family gone, Queens will never be the same place I knew as a child, the borough my mother bequeathed to me, inside and out—but the memories are there, and they're a comfort. I write these words from a desk in Philadelphia, where I now reside, only a couple of months after moving out of that apartment back in Sunnyside. I miss it there, and not just for the convenience of stores that carry any ethnic food ingredient I need, or the proximity to the airports, or the overhead rattle of the overcrowded, often foul-smelling, *wonderful* 7 train, filled with all its queers and single moms and diverse faces—but simply the feeling of knowing that no matter what, I'm a *Queens* girl, born and bred, and there, I truly belong.

Just last month, I returned to the crossroads of Junction and Northern, and spent a weekend in apartment 5V for the first time since I moved out. Down on Junction, there's a man who stands outside a cell phone store, screaming at the top of his lungs in Spanish, whose face I remembered very clearly. I hadn't been back there in over two years and yet, it was the exact same man, hollering about cell phones, as if no time had passed at all. When I first turned onto the street, outside of the Kent building, I saw the Junction Food Bazaar in the distance, which lives on the next block. The awning had a large sign attached to it that said WELCOME HOME in all caps, and I startled, wondering if the universe was speaking to me. As I got closer, I tried to find out what the sign meant, but had no luck—just a sign hanging from an awning, for no other reason than to welcome me home; to remind me just where home is.

85-11 Avon Street

Julia Alvarez

In 1963, after three years of renting other people's apartments and houses, my parents set about finding our very own house in this country.

The first idea was Brooklyn. Papi had finally gotten his license and opened his own office on Graham Avenue, in an area with lots of Spanish-speakers. ALVAREZ CENTRO MEDICO was a narrow, windowless walk-in clinic, where all payment was in cash and young nurses with dubious diplomas ran *loterías* and numbers games, along with giving shots, taking x-rays, and offering advice on just about anything.

We spent various Sunday afternoons driving around Papi's office, the whole family packed in the car, the four sisters in the back seat having finally settled on who would get the windows this time. I'd stare out at the littered streets, the tenement buildings bracketed by fire escapes, the teensy intermittent parks, trying to imagine a life here. I kept coming up with a blank.

Mami must have too, if for different reasons. What was Papi thinking? This was not a safe area for his daughters. The schools were terrible. Crime, drugs, muggings. She had not escaped a dictatorship and come all the way to the United States to be shot at by gangsters and addicts.

Instead she settled on Queens, close enough to everything: a mere twenty-five minutes from the city on the E or the F train, a half-hour commute for Papi to his office; close to both airports so it'd be easy to come and go to the Dominican Republic now that the dictator had been assassinated; blocks away from the elementary school, Immaculate Conception, and the high school, Mary Louis Academy, so that even if we could not be among other Dominicans, we could at least be among Catholics.

Queens, like the queen, Mami would quip, pleased with herself at being able to make a word play in English. It was as if my mother had finally found what immigrants come to America looking for. But what most appealed to her about our new neighborhood was not that it reflected those admirable American virtues of equality and opportunity. What most delighted her were the trappings of privilege and pedigree. The house was in Jamaica *Estates*, a tony area where most of the residents (except us) were a couple of generations removed from having come here. The streets were wide, tree-lined, with Anglophile names like Eton and Somerset and Wexford, as opposed to the streets on the other side of Hillside Avenue, in plain Jamaica, that were just numbered—179th Street, 189th Place, 90th Avenue—with houses lined up in rows, shoulder to shoulder, as if waiting their turn to cross over and get names, lawns, and faux British addresses.

85-11 Avon Street, our new home, looked just like all the other houses around it: a standard red brick with the requisite bay window and a little decorative balcony you couldn't really stand in, on the second floor. "Ay, Mami," we complained. "*Tan aburrida*." So boring. We had seen much more exciting houses with attics and wraparound porches and libraries with ladders for reaching the high shelves, but this small, straightforward residence had nothing to distinguish it. That was the beauty of this place, my mother argued: the house blended in with the others, which made it eminently re-sellable.

We hadn't even moved in, and she was already plotting our exit!

Given that it was a good neighborhood, as my mother would remind my father whenever he complained after an especially long commute from Brooklyn, it's surprising that one of the first things she did was install an alarm system. Every window and door was wired. The worst of it was that on those early mornings when you forgot to turn it off before opening the door to collect the paper, the alarm would not only wake up the neighbors, but it also rang down at the police station. Half-asleep yourself, you'd have to rush in and dial the special number to cancel the call from 85-11 Avon Street. More often than not, the alert had already gone out to some police car cruising the neighborhood, and the cops would show up, lights flashing. I'd run back outside, apologizing profusely, while up and down the street, neighbors watched, no doubt thinking that these new immigrants did not belong here among established, law-abiding, quiet citizens.

But there is a saying in Dominican Spanish: *un clavo saca otro clavo*, one nail drives out another; that is: a new worry takes your mind off the old one. A few months after our arrival, a black family moved in across the street. Overnight, it seemed our neighbors stopped worrying about us because here was a bigger problem. No matter that the father was a professional, the superintendent of something. The point was that our houses would be worth nothing when we went to resell. This was the commentary my mother reported from neighbors who, for the first time since our arrival, were including her in their conversations.

There were rumors about a burning cross on their lawn, telephoned threats. Now the cop cars regularly patrolled our street. Never had we been safer, I pointed out to my mother, who was on the fence about how to feel about our new neighbors. By now with teenagers in the house who held her to account for every hypocritical stance she took or inanity she uttered, she didn't dare come out and say that she had something against the color of their skin. What about some of our relatives back home? What about all men being created equal? What about the prejudice we ourselves had encountered in this country—kids calling us spics, a lady in the grocery store who overheard us talking in Spanish telling us to go back to where we had come from.

"It's not about their color," Mami defended herself. "Your father worked very hard so we could buy this house. It's not me making the rules in this country!"

In July of 1964, those who were making the laws in this country passed the Civil Rights Act. Segregation was illegal. But by then, the corner house was again on the market. Our new neighbors were moving out. There hadn't really been an incident to drive them away, all of the rumors having turned out to be just that. But maybe the family had picked up the noxious vibes from all around, from the Lauderbachs and the Ehmers, the Callahans and O'Caseys, Castelluccis and Peregrinis, Dillers and Steinways, and yes, the Alvarezes.

I include our name, even if my family wasn't responsible for the rules in this country. We could have made, if not a big difference, a dozen tiny ones. Mami could have gone across the street with one of her excellent flans or a potted azalea. Papi was never around, true, leaving early to avoid traffic and coming home late after making house calls. But on one of those rare Sundays when he got home early, he could have crossed over and introduced himself.

My own opportunity came one morning when I went out to collect the newspaper. Across the street, the front door opened. A young girl about my age stepped out, followed by her father, both of them headed to the car in their driveway that he must have gone out earlier and started, warming it up for her. Idling at the curb, ready to follow them, was a cop car.

After several months of defending an abstraction, here they were. But when the girl looked up, the expression on her face was of such anger and hurt, I could physically feel myself blown back by its repelling force. The hand I was about to wave dropped to my side. My mother had gotten her wish: we had blended in with all the other families on the street.

Forty-three years later, I find myself again in Queens, attending a *quinceañera* in Maspeth. Driving down Metropolitan Avenue, I can't believe this is the same place I knew as a young teen, of quinceañera age myself. Multiculturalism has hit: the storefronts reflect cultures from around the world—Irish, Italian, German, Chinese, Indian, Greek, and many Latinos of all races from all the Americas. In fact, later reading up on Queens, I'm not surprised to learn that according to the 2000 census, 48 percent of its inhabitants are foreign born.

But Jamaica Estates is as quiet, groomed, buttoned down as I remember it. It's as if the whole neighborhood has been packed away in mothballs. I half expect to see the young girl I was, opening the door of 85-11 Avon, triggering the alarm, racing in to beat the cops from driving up to our house, confirming our neighbors' qualified opinion of us.

I park in front of our old house, feeling that shock of seeing a place that for years has only existed in my memory. Nothing has changed here either—no additions, no new deck or wraparound porch. How many families have owned the house since my parents sold it twenty-five years ago, I wonder, the resale value climbing because of its eminent virtue, the opportunity to blend in with everyone else? But who is this *everyone else* now? I haven't seen a soul on the streets, no one mowing a lawn, or collecting the paper. Surely, Jamaica Estates has felt some impact from the enormous demographic tidal waves that have washed in, only miles away?

I decide to climb out of my car and ring the doorbell. Just mention to the new owners that I once lived here. Maybe they'll invite me in for a brief nostalgic tour of the old homestead, the standard fare of rooms looking even smaller than I remember, the living room where we were not allowed to sit, the dining room where we only ate when it was a holiday, the kitchen with the alcove where we were crowded around the small table, the two tiny bedrooms my sisters and I shared, the basement, where we hung out, plotting our escape into the American freedoms our parents refused to let us enjoy.

No one answers. But as I turn to go, I hear the lock clicking, a chain slipping, and the door opens a crack. Peering out is a young Asian woman from a country I can't guess. Her face is so full of suspicion and fear. I'm actually surprised she dared open the door at all. At her side is a small boy looking at me curiously.

"I used to live here," I try explaining. I could give her more details: how my parents moved from here, finally returning to the Dominican Republic, the place they still considered home after forty-three years in this country. The math of it all often overwhelms me. That so many years have passed. That roots can go so deep they defy time: the home where you are born being the place you have to go to die.

But the woman before me is shaking her head either to let me know she understands no English or that she wants nothing to do with me. Her little boy begins to cry. Am I that scary? I'm not carrying a weapon or even a sheath of pamphlets promoting some religion or political party or line of cosmetics. Only my car keys and a head full of memories.

"Okay, thanks," I tell her, lifting a hand to show I'm harmless, unarmed, and most importantly, about to go.

It's only once I am safely a few steps away from the door that I get to hear her voice, saying something in a language I don't speak. But I understand the warning in her tone; leave, or she will call the police.

I climb back in my car and make my getaway before the cops come, and I again have to apologize for creating a nuisance at 85-11 Avon Street.

To Bridge: The Spaces Between, Behind, and Around Us

Buzz Poole

Maybe you just see a bridge: masonry towers 250 feet high, a rust-colored arch more than 1,000 feet long running between them; 90,000 tons of steel; 450,000 cubic yards of concrete reinforced by 5,000 tons of steel rods; 340,000 rivets; the work of approximately 140 men per day from 1912 until 1917. Just how closely are you looking?

When Gustav Lindenthal, a legend of bridge building, engineered the Hell Gate Bridge, he was looking close enough that when the two halves of the arch were lowered to form a whole, the first try was only 5/16 of an inch off the mark.

Easy and close, like men of Astoria on Steinway Street—standing around the bocce court, pacing back and forth tracking the balls, smoking, sipping deli coffee out of paper cups, constant Greek chattering. Questioning. The low grey clouds might snow. But the game is what they see: the ability to roll balls with precision and finesse, not quite touching but close enough, like Lindenthal's design.

But then there is a crowding, men shoulder to shoulder around the balls.

"I don't know."

"I don't know."

The English surprises. They pass the phrase between one another. The Greek continues, as they discuss which ball is closest to the jack, the small ball around which the game orbits. A question of proximity, a surprisingly subjective term—like *home*, especially here in Queens where the Hell Gate Bridge, a jeweled ring on the borough's knuckle, spans the East River, bringing distance home and taking home the distance. Home is a replacement.

Don't let the name fool you. "Hell Gate" has nothing to do with how the bridge now looks, glowing majestic and mythical in the evening hours as the sun descends into the teeth of Manhattan's skyline. The action on the bridge today is limited—only a few trains on any given day, neglected and forgotten by most outside the neighborhood, no match for the youthful verve of a newcomer like its younger sibling, the RFK. Now it is more like a reluctant ornament for Astoria Park, loud with children playing and cars cruising, the hillside sloping toward the East River. None of this factored into Lindenthal's intention. What he built inspired the Sydney Harbor Bridge; it was the greatest and longest in the world, for a time.

But the color—Hell Gate Red, they call it—that was an afterthought, instigated by Senator Daniel Patrick Moynihan, brought to fruition in 1996 with a $55 million paint job. Credit Dutch navigator Adriaen Block and sunken ships for the bridge's name. The Dutch word *Hellegat* referred to the East River (technically a tidal straight, meaning it doesn't flow, per se) and, in particular, the harrowing passage between Astoria and Ward Island. It sunk hundreds of ships, including the frigate *Hussar*, which went down in 1780 with millions of dollars of cargo. They say most of it is still down there today. There must be old bones, too. This is also the site of the city's deadliest maritime disaster. In June 1904 an overwhelming majority of the 1,300 members of St. Mark's German Lutheran Church perished when a steamer, the *General Slocum*, caught fire. The people either burned or drowned.

The only way to tame the tides riled up by rocks was to blast with dynamite. So in 1876 the Army Corps of Engineers set off what was, at the time, the largest detonation of explosives in the world. Not too long thereafter the railroad replaced the ships, though nothing replaced the rocks, or the lives.

The Pennsylvania Railroad's ability to freight cargo throughout the Northeast and west to Lake Erie came to be with the construction of this bridge. It is appropriate that Queens is the borough upon which this feat stands, supporting tracks that rise up and course along viaducts that pass over the Hell Gate Bridge and into the Bronx. It makes sense when considering Queens today, its populations as in transit as they are permanent, as new as they are rooted in generations. And like the bridge's history, and its more recent paint job that everyone assumes is as old as the bridge, the citizens of Queens have their own histories, their own backgrounds that get a fresh paint job for the sake of their new home, though sometimes the alterations go deeper than the surface.

They say that if you can't find it in New York City, it doesn't exist. Plenty of what you might go looking for is found in Queens; its inhabitants bring what they want and leave the rest at home. Queens is a potent tincture of America in that respect; you can have everything you may want and not bother with the rest. In Elmhurst, the Queens Center Mall—all you'd expect from an American mall—provides translation in more than forty-five languages.

The real-estate agent hails from Cusco, Peru, land of tourists on the march to Machu Picchu. The life his mother maintains is not for him, though he never stops sending money, never stops earning because he never stops working. First he went to France and worked in kitchens, learned enough of the language to fake his way through, but then America beckoned. Offers from friends he didn't know he had girded his next move, that move to Queens. He worked in more kitchens, catering, making more friends and tooling his English to use it when he had to, though he never really wanted to; what he wanted to do was make money. They didn't have enough in Peru. The wife and daughters needed it too, and he wanted to provide it, provide everything. And he did, thanks to all of the work. Hence the English, and the real estate license. But no matter how many $500,000 properties he sells, the fear of not having enough still motivates him to take catering gigs, a good night's sleep nowhere as important as taking care of his family. He dozes off watching movies with his daughter on the couch. Her disability forces her to be at home most of the time with Mom, family, hired help. But none of them compare to Daddy, and they all know it. And while his SUV and natty suits and sweater vests smack of America, there is nothing of it in his demeanor: he's always running late for appointments, taking time for *café y pan* between every open house, making unannounced late-night visits to get paperwork signed that he forgot about earlier in the day, efficiency and protocol secondary to the result of earning and providing for those he loves. He makes visits to Peru and France, thinking very little of those places now. He arrived in Queens years ago and it has become his home, his dream.

But there is the other side of all this, too. Bridges connect, but they can isolate if we cross and don't know how to return by the way we came. Or maybe we try to go back that same way but the destination is no longer the same. Maybe we aren't the same.

She's from Mexico, the bartender whose English is near flawless, like her beauty. The imperfections of her malaprops, and her mole, small eyes and nose—they become endearing. She only picked up the language when she made the journey to Queens as a teenager to be with her family. Since then, her brothers have moved—one back to Mexico, the other to Australia—and her father has died. She's been to film school, though she's never been to any of the countries that produced the artists she now worships. Sure, she can get a handle on Scorsese's New York. But Goddard's France, Kurosawa's Japan, Tarkovsky's Russia? No way. She wants to change that, as if the lack of experience is a bad habit, but an inevitable return to Mexico haunts her. How does she go back and face the still living mother of her now dead father? What do you say of the country that lets you forget where you came from? What do you say of the country that makes you think of all other countries but your own? And which country is yours anymore? Home is a variable.

There are two sides to every bridge. But those two sides cannot always be assimilated. They can never be the same.

We are now over the Atlantic Ocean, somewhere between New York and London on a flight that will continue to Mumbai. A man fishes for conversation, offering chocolate as bait.

"You are going to India?"

"No, only to London."

"India is a beautiful country. You visit someday and stay with me? Yes, yes, here is my card."

"Thank you; that's very kind."

"Please, the chocolate is too much for me alone. I bought it for my son."

"You don't want to give away a gift for your son."

The bait has worked.

"My son didn't want it. Three months I have been in Jackson Heights, staying with family waiting for my son to see me. You wonder where he was? Manhattan, busy with school. He would not let me visit him and in three months, he only came to see me in Queens twice. Do you know Queens?"

I tell him I live there; his tone goes from friendly to approving.

"Do you ignore your family, too? He is busy with school, studying, but I worry he works too hard. Family is everything, at least where we come from. But it is not everything to him anymore. Not now, not after living in this place. It is a place that makes you believe the rest of the world doesn't exist. That the world is here."

The man points at his lap, as if we are still in New York, on the ground rather than high above water on an invisible bridge. But it is appropriate because the tides of ambition that swell the city have long-reaching effects, something akin to the relationship between the moon and oceans.

There is a convergence of train lines at the Jackson Heights-Roosevelt Avenue station in Queens that makes Times Square seem downright tame. It's a place where the politics of space have devolved to anarchy, not violent but jostling. South Asians, Chinese, and Latinos are the majority; their prominence mirrors the world. The E train fills with them, as well as those from the projects in Jamaica and the more suburban settings of Queens that flirt with Long Island, plus the intrepid travelers who have just flown into JFK, worrying that New York doesn't look like it does in the movies. And then the coordinated screeds begin. From both ends of the car, dreadlocked African Americans speak of the moon landing's fraudulence: "It was fake. One giant leap, 'leap' just a new word for 'lie' . . . one giant lie for mankind."

Of course, almost all of us, no matter where our families hail from and when they decided to commit themselves to the great American experiment, are visitors to this land. Well before the arrival of European colonists, a trail passed along the East River right underneath where the Hell Gate stands today. A Native American village flourished at Pot Cove (a European naming based on discovered artifacts), a fact probably not lost on the Mohawk ironworkers recruited to help build the bridge. Perhaps they had been warring tribes, or perhaps they had never known of one another but here they were now, connected by bridging geography and time, preparing the land to be inhabited and used by almost everyone except the people who first called Queens home. The rest of us, we are living in lies, complicit in them.

In a den of commerce like New York City, making rain is all that matters. Say you can do it, and then do it; if you pull it off, nothing else matters. Lies happen. Here, then, is perhaps the perfect conclusion to Lindenthal's legacy and how that legacy is a tongue-and-groove fit with New York City, Queens in particular. The story goes that Lindenthal, upon arriving in the United States, boasted engineering degrees from institutes in his hometown of Brünn (now Brno, Czech Republic) and Vienna. He lied. According to a *New Yorker* feature about Lindenthal and the Hell Gate, neither of the polytechnic institutes had a record of a Gustav Lindenthal attending. His knowledge of bridges was self-taught, yet his creations still stand and support not just their own weight but traffic of the day. What he knew was right and true, and even though it was built on lies, those lies were the building blocks of his dreams.

It's a contemporary truth: what was once the greatest—whether a country or a bridge—becomes a memorial to the vagaries of time. But there is nothing anachronistic about the borough of Queens. More than Manhattan and Brooklyn, where image reigns supreme, people in Queens, especially the newest arrivals, adapt and re-adapt as they deem fit, selling the Qur'an on the sidewalk or wilting broccoli in the bodega; talking into a cell phone that's tucked into a *chador*; the Mandarin cacophony interjected with terms like *American Idol* and *Survivor*; a Queens patois based on the world that can only be understood in one place in the world: here. These are not the lies of advertising and America's media-driven mind; these are the things we do to survive.

Fierce tides and the traffic of industry were the East River's song. But now, multilingual soundtracks of ice cream trucks, revving engines and the flotsam of a consumer culture—broken glass, food wrappers, old, faded shoes and tires, slapping, tinkling, rattling—these are the new songs that rise and fall along the tidal shore: the songs of Queens.

Mournful, bronzed autumnal sunset draws out the day like taffy, long and unrelenting. Ambling amid rattling leaves, two men speak Greek. Their shoulders sway like the river; their punctuations flash like whitecaps. Squealing girls career their bicycles around the two who move along, seemingly oblivious. Perhaps they speak of the old country, a foreignness to them that seems impenetrable, far removed from the country they stroll through. But then the reality of their context is made clear as one of the men, in heavily accented English, says "freedom of speech," followed by laughter—the punch line to some joke.

Nothing remains the same, especially here, in this borough, this city, this country. The Hell Gate Bridge and Queens evolve with a nostalgic luster, these two testaments to human tenacity, even as they exist in our pixilated, networked age. A young couple, one on either side of their Subaru station wagon with an Obama bumper sticker; the man on the driver's side holding his iPhone at the woman on the passenger side, snapping her photo, but she looks more like posing for a mirror. He says, "Your new Facebook photo."

Just another kind of bridge, like the one that soars into the heavens on a March night; the planet Saturn is visible to the naked eye, a shimmering beacon in a clear sky, if you know where to look. Standing on the corner of Ditmars Boulevard and 29th Street in Astoria, Patrick, a neighborhood resident and a self-proclaimed "marble and tile guy," invites commuters returning home from work to view the planet's rings through his powerful telescope. His interest in astronomy goes back to his childhood, during which his father steeped him in mythology. The people that do stop are always glad they did, seeing the constellations in a way that reminds them of the movies. They learn that Saturn's quick trajectory across the lens is actually the result of the Earth's rotation. Home is movement.

Like the body language of ESL, gestures of recognition preempt the words in English—a head nod or a shoulder-stooping smile to a passerby who indeed passes without hearing the "It is good to see you" that eventually issues.

So many bridges connecting every inch of the globe and beyond, everything we can and cannot see, or want to see, bringing any of it, all of it, to you now, now, now in any language at any time. This is the reason to invest such local, national and human importance on this inorganic American structure, the Hell Gate Bridge, for America—and for that matter, Queens—is an artifice, an admirable borrowing and reinventing of the rest of the world.

There's a wind like you wouldn't believe that blows off the East River, buffing Queens. Its wintry bite cuts through clothes and in warmer months funnels a salty stench up your nose until you can taste it. The water ripples and gems and rare moments exist when today's soundtrack hushes, leaving only the sound of water, rustling trees, the approach of a train rumbling toward the Hell Gate Bridge. You can pretend the bridge has just opened, especially with the freight trains—the grandeur of slow movement pressed against the sky, metaphors awaiting words. You can pretend you are Gustav Lindenthal surveying his latest vision made real. What he saw in his mind is the life he realized. He is one of the lucky ones. Many find themselves in Queens, some standing right here under the bridge, trying to manifest their dreams. Some, like Lindenthal, succeed; many don't. Some spend their entire lives deciphering and translating their dreams. For some, even home is a dream.

Love and Shame

Margo Rabb

When I was in high school, it was an insult if anyone asked you, "Are you from *Queens?*"

It meant that those leopard-print leggings you wore were not a wise choice, you'd applied too much black eyeliner, your hair was styled too big, your fake gold earrings too large, and everything about you was cheesy, tacky, and unspeakably uncool.

My best friends and I strived to look like we lived in "the city." (That Queens was technically part of New York City didn't count.) Our high school, The Bronx High School of Science, drew kids from all five boroughs, and the pecking order seemed to be: Manhattan (the coolest); Bronx (points for proximity); Brooklyn (points for history); Staten Island (far away, exotic, and unknown); and Queens (the embarrassing cousin, who talks too loud and has food in her teeth).

My two best friends became my closest friends because we lived in Queens: it was hard not to become best friends when you rode the subway together for three hours a day. Our commute to school on the 7 and 4 trains took an hour and fifteen minutes each way when there were no delays; on the way home, the trip sometimes stretched to an hour and forty-five minutes, since we opted to take the D train, which was the train the cool kids took. (The coolest of the cool lived on the Upper West Side and in the Village.)

On weekends, my friends and I scraped our cash together and shopped at Andy's Chee-pees, Alice Underground, Unique, and Antique Boutique on Broadway, culling together our sleek, secondhand, mostly black, Manhattan-worthy wardrobes, until our Manhattan friends agreed: we didn't look like we were from Queens.

Other rules of inter-borough friendships:

1. You cannot expect your Manhattan friends to come visit you in Queens.

2. All social life will inevitably center around your Manhattan friends' apartments.

3. The one time your Manhattan friends do come visit, you will probably feel embarrassment and shame, even if you can't pinpoint what exactly is wrong with your neighborhood.

I hadn't always felt ashamed of my borough: as a kid I'd loved it. I'd lived in Sunnyside since I was born, six houses down from where my father had grown up. In our living room we had a painting my grandfather made of the alley behind our house, before it was paved, with ancient-looking cars dotting the street. I loved walking home from P.S. 11, my elementary school, down Skillman Avenue, the Empire State Building looming in the distance, looking so close that you could run your fingers down its silky glass. My friends and I'd buy slices of pizza for fifty cents at Rosario's, where Rosario himself knew all our names, and penny candy from the newsstand across the street, where they sold newspapers in ten different languages. I loved all the foods: the Turkish grocery's fresh baklava and spinach pies, the Mexican bakery's empanadas, the Chinese bakery's red bean buns, and sweet rice cakes at the Korean grocery store. I loved the snowy winters when we played in the middle of the street, laughing at stalled buses and reveling in the sudden hushed quiet. I loved Sunnyside Gardens park, the wooden jungle gym that my father, an engineer, had helped design and build; the tiny two-foot-deep swimming pool; the hidden courtyards of Sunnyside Gardens that seemed full of secrets: mulberry trees dropping sweet, ripe fruit, a hutch of baby bunnies in a neighbor's yard, weeping willows and magnolias and maples. I thought the squat brick houses were beautiful, with the snow collecting in their eaves, and the giant trees arching over the street, their roots cracking up the cement sidewalks.

Still, it wasn't exactly a bucolic idyll. When I was nine my friend Leslie and I were walking to her house when a man approached us in the street, his penis hanging out the fly of his pants. He pointed at it and said, "You like?" We giggled and ran. He wasn't the only flasher I'd see

as a child—other incidents followed, including a car pulling up, trying to
get me to climb inside, and in seventh grade, as my friend Maya and I
walked to junior high, a gun was pulled on a group of teens twenty feet
away from us. We hid behind a car. But at the time, these things never
seemed that big a deal—even my parents never made a tremendous fuss
over them, as I imagine parents might now. You learned how to behave
in the city: aware of yourself at all times, always ready to flee.

But throughout my teens, the love of my neighborhood became buried
by my shame of it, and I couldn't wait to move away. Do all teenagers feel
this frustration with their hometowns, and that's why they're spurred to
leave? The shame persisted into my early twenties; when I was in graduate
school in Tucson, Arizona, my French professor boyfriend came home
with me on a visit, and his disdain of the neighborhood was clear. He
needed to buy T-shirts and socks, and so I took him to ABC Variety, a
discount store on Queens Boulevard. He flicked through the clothing in
cheap bins, complaining that the store smelled like fish (mysteriously, it
always did), frowning, bewildered that there were no cafés or restaurants
like in Manhattan, no good place to get a glass of wine. It wasn't the New
York City he'd expected. When we ate dinner with a friend's boyfriend,
who didn't know that I was from Queens, the boyfriend blurted, "Why
are the airports here in *the worst part of the city*? People fly into New
York and think it's this armpit, this god-awful place till they finally get
over the bridge to Manhattan."

The buried shame persisted in the years I lived away from New York.
Then, when I was twenty-six, I came back. My father had died of a heart
attack. My mother had died seven years before that, and suddenly my
sister and I became the owners of our Sunnyside home.

We had to decide what to do—to keep it or sell it. My sister already
had a job and a life out west; I'd just finished graduate school and wasn't
sure where to live next. Our father's estate needed to be settled and the
house badly needed repairs, so I decided to move back to Sunnyside for
a while and sort things out.

Living in Sunnyside again, by myself, I felt this mixed tangle of fierce
love and aching memory. The confusing shame I'd felt as a teenager came
rushing back. I was single then, and dating, and once more I faced that
Queens stigma whenever I told a Manhattan man where I lived (and
all our dates inevitably took place in Manhattan). And yet my love for
Sunnyside returned more fervently than it ever had; finally, after living
away for years, I appreciated how unique our neighborhood was, how
even Manhattan didn't have Turkish and Greek and Irish and Mexican
and Korean and Chinese food shops all within blocks of each other, or

an elementary school with kids from dozens of different countries, or a library with book sections in Bengali, Gujarati, Hindi, Turkish, Korean, Spanish, Romanian, and Chinese. Neighbors brought food after my father died, left gifts, looked out for me. My sister and I both realized how much we loved our neighborhood, where we'd lived off and on now for nearly thirty years, and how it would break our hearts to leave it for good.

I lived in the house for a year. Finally, my sister and I decided to sell it. But it wasn't the shame that made me decide to sell—it was the fierce love, too strong and overpowering, too rich with memory, too close, that I couldn't escape. Every time I walked down Skillman Avenue, or waited on the 7 train platform, staring at the skyline, I wasn't only myself, but the self I'd been at five and ten and fifteen and twenty, and there was no escaping those memories, or the ever-present grief.

In the years since, I've often regretted our decision to sell that house. Even now, ten years later, I often dream that I'm living there again. The dream is nearly always the same: our house is much larger, with beautiful open rooms with secret passageways and gardens stretching for miles. At the end of the dream it dawns on me that I did leave it, it's no longer ours, and I need to find a way to get it back. And then I wake up. But in those seconds between dream life and waking life, I know one thing: I can't ever leave it, I haven't left, it will always be my home.

Waiting for Big Bird

Marcy Dermansky

Jonathan jumps up from his seat, knocking over his mug of coffee when Mona tells him she thinks she is in labor. They are having brunch at Café Bar. It is one of their favorite things to do.

"You aren't due for two weeks," he says.

Mona agrees. She is not due for another two weeks, and she cannot be sure that what she feels is labor, because she has never been in labor before.

"I'm pretty sure," Mona says.

They are sitting at an outdoor table across the street from the Kaufman Astoria Studios. The sun is shining. They had the day ahead of them, plans to go home and clean the apartment. They have ordered the same dishes they always order: the Mediterranean scramble for Jonathan and the herb omelet with goat cheese for Mona. Jonathan's scrambled eggs are swimming in spilt coffee. This is his first coffee of the day. Mona is afraid her husband will cry. She motions for the waiter.

It is a useless gesture. They are sitting outside. Fabio just served their food. He went back inside. It could be minutes before he returns.

"I have this fantasy that one day Big Bird will come walking down the street," Mona says. She closes her eyes. Labor. It was inevitable. "Big Bird will come to Café Bar," she says. "And he orders a frappé."

Mona has said this before, many times. It is a line that has long ago ceased to be clever, though Mona has never stopped wishing for Big Bird. *Sesame Street* is produced at the Kaufman Astoria Studios; a cameo appearance by the tall, yellow creature is not in the realm of the impossible.

"I saw Denzel Washington here once," Jonathan says.

"You did? You never told me that."

"They were filming that Pelham movie."

"I can't believe you didn't tell me that." Mona is surprised by how angry this makes her. Her forehead is covered in sweat. She is not supposed to go into labor two weeks early. She has work still to get done. The edits on her book are due. The baby was supposed to come late. "Did you see John Travolta?"

"Only Denzel Washington. He was wearing a dark suit. He ordered a beer and the halloumi sandwich."

Mona has never once seen a celebrity at Café Bar. She has lived with Jonathan in Astoria for six years, longer than she has lived anywhere else in her adult life. Their two-bedroom apartment is too small for a baby. The cramped office they share would be the baby's room, but Mona and Jonathan are writers who work from home. They need that office. They fight over who gets to sit in that office. They have made a schedule. For years, they have talked about moving, but somehow, they never move. They don't have enough money.

When Mona tells people that she lives in Astoria, she is surprised by the most frequent response. *I love the Greek restaurants,* she is told again and again. Maybe that is true. Maybe everyone in Manhattan loves to make a yearly pilgrimage to Astoria for the authentic Greek food experience, but the truth is Mona never goes to these restaurants. The grilled fish, the wine, the fried cheese, and the lemon potatoes—a meal for two is never less than seventy dollars. Except Uncle Georges. The local dive is cheaper, especially the house wine, served in a tall carafe and poured into what looks like shot glasses. Mona always walks out of Uncle Georges pleasantly drunk. Except, of course, she has not been drunk in a long while. Mona does not think Astoria will be a good place to raise her baby. She thinks that it is ugly. There are not enough green places.

There is, Mona knows, Astoria Park. And Mona likes this park. Other summers, when she was not pregnant, when she was more inclined to walk ten blocks to the N train, ride it two stations, and then walk another half mile still to the park, she swam laps there in the enormous swimming pool designed by Robert Moses. Mona loved to swim in that pool, watch the sun set over the East River. But as far as parks go, it's faster to take the subway to Central Park. Where Mona lives, it's all ugly architecture and cement.

"Oh," Mona says.

Mona is in labor. She is having another contraction.

"Okay. I think this might be painful."

She looks at Jonathan, trying to gauge from the expression on his face how she should feel. He is looking anxiously at the door, waiting for his coffee. They had known this was going to happen. They are almost forty years old. They are not children. At this particular moment in time, Mona doesn't want to panic. Mona wants to eat her omelet. She also wants to go home and pack her bag. She has been told, repeatedly, to pack this bag for her stay in the hospital. She has continuously put it off, though, still needing her toothbrush, her toothpaste, her favorite pair of pajamas. Mona has been unwilling to pack these items. She has also been busy, editing her book.

"I don't believe Denzel Washington ordered the halloumi sandwich," Mona says. "You are making that up."

"Maybe I made that part up." Jonathan smiles.

Mona loves him for that, for the smile.

Fabio, the waiter, has finally come back outside and is on his way to their table. Of all the waiters at Café Bar, he is Mona's favorite. Mona feels grateful.

"Can we get some more coffee?" Mona asks him. "And the check, please? As soon as you can?"

"Already?" Fabio expertly refills Jonathan's empty mug. He pulls out a rag from his back pocket and begins to wipe the table. "Don't worry," he says, lifting Jonathan's plate of ruined eggs, and then wiping away the coffee that pooled beneath it. "I'll get you another order. It will take no time."

"We have no time," Jonathan says.

Jonathan pours milk in his coffee, brings the mug to his lips, closes his eyes. Mona looks down, again, at her food. She picks out a piece of asparagus from her home fries with her fingers. Mona eats the asparagus and wishes that she hadn't. She isn't hungry. She might need to throw up. They will, of course, still have to pay for this meal. Café Bar isn't cheap. Mona knows she shouldn't be worrying about wasting thirty dollars when she is about to have a baby, but she is.

Also, Mona has changed her mind. She does not want to have a baby. She knows this is the stupidest possible thing to think, but that is what she is thinking. She hasn't even packed her bag. Clearly, she is unequipped for what lies ahead. Mona blinks. She considers her breakfast, virtually untouched. When she goes to the hospital, she knows they won't let her eat. She will probably be in labor for a long time. Mona never took a birthing class. All of the classes took place in Brooklyn or Manhattan and Mona did not have time for such a class. Mona cuts off a tiny piece of omelet with the edge of her fork, but she doesn't eat it. A bead of sweat drops from her chin onto the table.

"Are you okay?" Fabio asks.

"No," Mona says.

"She's in labor," Jonathan says and then takes another gulp of coffee. "We have to go to the hospital, but we need to go home first. And pick up the bag."

"We didn't pack our bag," Mona says.

"We need to go home and pack it," Jonathan agrees.

"Can we do that?" Mona asks him.

Their apartment is six blocks away. That seems especially far. Mona, of course, cannot change her mind. She is going to have a baby, and she is going to bring the baby home to live with them in their not-big-enough apartment that is next door to the auto repair shop. This is what is going to happen. There are, of course, other babies that live on the same street, who seem to grow up just fine, in Astoria, without anything green. Identical twins, beautiful Indian girls almost always dressed in the same clothes live next door. They were toddlers when Jonathan and Mona first moved in, and now they are big girls. Mona smiles at these girls and they smile at Mona. After six years of living next door, watching them grow, she does not know their names.

They still have not moved from their table. Jonathan and Fabio are watching Mona, solicitous, but also useless.

Mona looks across the street, still hoping for Big Bird. And if not Big Bird, she'll take Oscar the Grouch. Or Snuffleupagus, Big Bird's imaginary friend, except, apparently, he is no longer invisible. Or Cookie Monster. Mona would be happy with Cookie Monster.

"I didn't even know you were pregnant," Fabio says.

This unexpected observation makes Mona strangely happy. She is plenty pregnant, eight and a half months pregnant, but her face has stayed the same. She has been swimming laps the entire time. Not at Astoria Park, but at the cheap Russian gym with the indoor pool. That is something thing Mona loves about her neighborhood, the gym, which is just around the corner from Café Bar.

"A boy or a girl?" Fabio asks.

"A girl," Mona says. "A girl."

They have picked a name, though Mona is not sure she likes it. Neither is Jonathan. A name is a big decision. Mona has trouble giving titles to her short stories. Again, Mona feels panic. She is not ready to have a baby. She looks at Fabio. He is a good waiter, efficient and friendly. He is kind. If the baby were a boy, she could name him Fabio.

"We have to pay you," Mona tells him, but she does not move to get her wallet. She feels that pain come back around, smashing her flat like an ocean wave.

Fabio waves his hand.

"Go," he says. "Go have a baby."

Mona looks at Jonathan. Go have a baby? Is that what they are supposed to do?

"I'm ready," he says.

His cup of coffee is empty. He puts his hand on Mona's. She looks into his eyes. He is ready.

"Breathe," Jonathan says.

Thinking on the N

Susan Y. Chi

I woke up beneath the raised platform of the Ditmars stop in Astoria, Queens. It was about 5:00 a.m. I rejoined the world as a snow angel in a puffy, red parka, my arms and legs imprinted in white powder as the N train rumbled overhead. I got up and walked to Laura's apartment. I'd moved out a year ago but often went by like I still lived there. It was comforting to both of us, I think. We met freshman year in high school. L.A. was far away. And here we were, best friends in a wonderful place with trains and real winters. Laura has thick black hair that she used to dye purple when we were kids; that morning she combed it into a slick ponytail. She stepped into plaid galoshes, wrapped a belt around a shearling coat, and pulled on a pair of leather gloves stitched with tasteful brass studs. She worked in midtown at a magazine. I poured hot water into a mug of Jameson as I watched her get ready, though mostly, I was trying to remember how I ended up sleeping in the snow. There was this scratch on my face, too; it was deeper than it looked. I must have cut myself with my keys when I fell.

I remember Astoria in summertime clearly: cement gardens drenched in yellow glaze, candy-striped awnings shielding old people from the sun, and plastic tumblers wiggling like jellies as a smoggy heat wave swept by. I was twenty-three when I arrived. At night, bulbs lit up along my walks home and, in spite of the teenagers kissing on the corners or the old people smoking long-ashed cigarettes in the heat, the streets seemed perfectly barren, as if it were only me and the stone angels, glowing in a

halo of lawn lights. That summer, our place on Ditmars Avenue and 36th
Street could've been New York City, for all I knew. And for all I knew,
Laura and I would always be happy. It never crossed my mind that second,
third, and fourth chances didn't last forever; even riding the building's old
gated elevator was as exciting as disappearing in a stranger's car.

If you ask, people will usually tell you about the Greek diners and
pastry shops, the Bohemian Beer Garden on 24th Avenue, the hookah
joints and gold-plated restaurants on Steinway—but to me, Astoria is
simply a place of old people and young people. By old people, I mean the
seniors citizens shuffling in their apartments with their fat cats and dirty
dogs. I mean the red-eyed elderly, adjusting air conditioning units that
blow dust all over their silver spoons and napkin dispensers. And as for
the young, forget the teenagers and the grade-school kids—imprinted in
my memory are those of us who met up, crowding the Ditmars station,
ready for the N to take us into the city. We were transplants. We were
too excited to be here. And we looked it. In fact, I didn't meet a native
New York City club kid my entire first year. But what we had was this:
we stood on the open platform, the end of the line too, and over us the
sky was crystal, even at night, the clouds and rooftop gardens white and
hard-edged. It was like we'd fallen out from somewhere, maybe a hole in
the moon. I remember laughing and Laura's hair swishing over the small
of her back. We kissed friends we barely knew. We were a bouquet of
flowers amid the faint stench of old people; their faces, their newspaper
fans, pushed right up against us from countless windows, reflecting the
promised excitement of our evenings through cracked glass. Yet, back
then, even if such lonely shadows weighed upon me, you couldn't tell.
If you bought me a drink, told me I was pretty, you could see meadows
in my eyes. I had so many pills in my pocket. I could've built a rainbow.

After Hampshire College, Laura had moved to Queens with a handful
of friends in 1998. It was a time when adorable, buttoned-up liberal-arts
grads began sprouting through the cracks of Astoria, along with struggling
theater-types (whose well-trained voices and guttural enunciation always
surprised me at parties). I'm sure Greek families everywhere thought a
particular rain had passed through and that they'd missed it somehow. I
showed up two years after Laura and planned on staying with her indefinitely.

She wrote for the Asia Society, updated their Web site with economic
and political news from India—and she invited me to exhibit openings
and exclusive parties where I was introduced to the concept of donors:
roomfuls of impeccably dressed men who smiled effortlessly at my hemp
bracelets and seashell charms and terrycloth dresses. I was also introduced
to the concept of an investment bank. More than once I was asked by

a director or partner of a firm I'd not heard of to drop by an event I was too intimidated to attend. Back in our sweltering, rent-controlled apartment, the yellow walls and prewar molding made Laura and me feel even hotter. I have a distinct memory of a Camel soft pack holding a place in Marguerite Duras's *The Lover* at the foot of the couch. It was my favorite book. I understood the feeling of staring into the Mekong as if it carried you forever through your waking life; not that I'd ever floated down a river, but each day passed with a quiet murkiness that churned my emotions in a way I couldn't explain. As ice melted into our badly made gimlets, Laura would shake her head and tease knowingly about the men I was talking to.

"You can tell they're Asiaphiles, right? Sadly it's always the same guys flocking to these Asia Society events." She'd toss her hair and cool herself by beating her shirt. "It's not as if they *really* like you, which you should be grateful for, actually."

I'd crunch on ice, laughing it off.

The old lady who lived in the building across from us kept a birdcage by her window. Inside, a pair of white pigeons clucked and roosted. She'd reach in and feed them from the palm of her hand. Sometimes she'd take one out to hug it. Once, when I woke from an afternoon nap, her curtains were parted wider than usual, and as I sat up on the couch I heard wild fluttering. Behind her, pigeons flew all over her apartment. Her walls and tables dripped with white, wings and bodies and beady little eyes swooping all around her. It was feeding time. There seemed to be a pile of seeds by the bay window. Feathers floated like snowflakes. I didn't want to look but I couldn't turn away, and when the old lady caught me she simply stared at me with happy eyes and waved with a glass of milk in her hand.

I tried not to let her ruin the view from our living room: fire escapes, square gardens, clotheslines, and freestyle graffiti flowing from building to building—it was as much part of my fantasy as the Chelsea Hotel. At night the Triborough and Hell Gate Bridges hummed gently like my young, worry-free life.

The beer garden was walking distance from the apartment, so we did go. In its cement courtyard, we'd gather around plastic tables the same way we did on the N train platform. Umbrellas swayed and napkins flew. Along a brick wall were a line of BBQ grills, and you could buy a sausage or pork chop for three dollars or cook your own if you got there early enough. Laura reminisced about her year in Prague before college with friends who had also gone. The more we drank from the vast selection of

Czech beers and the more Slavic chatter swirled around us, the faster the Mekong flowed when I closed my eyes, and I knew things were already being made into a memory as I breathed.

For a short time, the owner opened a club downstairs. It was a joke if you weren't Greek or Eastern European, but if you were a person who went inside the bar instead of sitting in the garden—inside where it was dark and where nobody wanted to enjoy summer—and walked down a few steps, you'd walk right into strobe lights and Euro disco and white jeans and cut-off sleeves and feathered hair. It was like the Berlin Wall melting on acid. I'd tell my friends I was going to the bathroom and wander into the club and if Laura came down to get me, I'd tell her not to worry. In fact, I was staying. She'd smirk at the kitsch. "Just be careful, Susan," she'd say. That meant, "Don't get so drunk you forget our address again."

I jumped into the crowd and danced and people let me into their circles, because by two in the morning, nobody cared about shit. I'd knock a pitcher of beer onto the floor and people would laugh. Some girls were barely of age, and some women were in their forties. The men all seemed older, but they danced, filled the place with body odor, and eventually we'd all stumble into a vinyl booth.

I asked a woman once if she went to clubs in the city and she said, "Why? There they rip you off. Here, party is better!" Her lips were frosty pink and her eyebrows penciled in. Her name was Mirha. She was with her cousin, Ermina. They both cleaned rooms at the Pierre. "Next time you stay in hotel don't forget, housekeepers see everything. Some guests, you know what they leave in bathrooms? Blood, shit on towels—men like girls do sex in the butt. Listen, I don't care what anyone do—but use toilet paper, clean yourself, my God!"

We passed a joint around the booth. Then Mirha took my hand and pulled me off the seat; we danced cheek to cheek until she spun me around and we fell onto a disco block that glowed square colors like a Rubik's Cube. She dug a wallet of photos from her purse.

"Can you imagine? I was just sixteen when I get married. Thirty-five I am now. Look, that is me." She pointed to a photo of her wedding in Albania. Her young, pale skin was as smooth as an egg. She stood in front of a gilded Muslim temple, a breeze blowing across her wedding gown. It was white, woven with gold thread and sequins, and tapered into harem pants at the ankles. "Here's Ermina. Only, what, twelve? Beautiful, eh?" Ermina was tiny in the wrinkled picture, even though they she was a tall, broad-shouldered woman now. She stood with twelve other bridesmaids, blue-eyed and stringy-haired, holding a headdress that looked like a fez flowing with veils. "Three hundred guests I had at my wedding," Mirha continued, shaking her head. "Imagine that."

I remember leaving the club one night with my neighbor Colin. He lived next door in our hall. He hoisted me out of a booth by the elbow.

"Laura's looking for you. They're all going into the city."

"You guys go without me. I'll meet up later."

Colin handed me a glass of water. He went upstairs. Then, after a few minutes, he came back down. "They're gone," he said. "I'm hanging around. You look like someone should be making sure you're all right."

Colin was from Galway and had this Gaelic cross tattooed to his arm. He could pass for a redheaded James Dean. He lifted a whiskey to his lips like a real drinker.

"How's your band?" I asked, yelling through the disco. My heart was beating from the fever of dancing and the drinks and the mix of Xanax, Valium, Wellbutrin, and Prozac—medications prescribed to me at one time or another, not to be taken together, obviously. My heart was also beating because Colin was there. His whole life was about his music. You could hear it in his voice when he talked. But every so often, he'd throw in an offhanded comment about turning thirty-three.

"We haven't 'made it' yet, but we will."

"It has to happen," I said, all slurry. "You guys are too good to fail."

"Right, *fail*. Well, we would've broken up by now if we didn't believe in ourselves. It's like, if you don't, no one else will."

I toasted to that. It was the end of summer. I was burning up. I'm not sure when it clicked, but I learned to make every night into New Year's Eve. I could even convince strangers we were celebrating the end of the world. I took joy in knowing I could throw my life away and the next day, nothing would happen to me. And I'd do it again because being drunk at sunrise was the best show on earth.

I remember Colin walking me home. The morning light fell on the angels. Even then, at the break of dawn, some old lady came out to water a fountain with a green hose. We sat against a gate a few apartments down when I started feeling queasy.

"Why didn't you go with the rest of them?" I asked.

Colin shrugged. "I didn't feel like it. I've done the drill a hundred times already."

I was glad he stayed. It was wonderful to sit out there with him.

"Nobody goes to a bar to get drunk," Colin said in a low voice. He looked sad and hopeful and wise. "They go to fall in love. I still want to think you can find it in one night."

I'd sleep in Colin's apartment a few times, and although Laura dreamed next to us on the other side of his bedroom wall, she never suspected a thing until I finally told her.

"How'd you do it?" she said. She looked ready to cry, and that surprised me; I wondered what else Laura was holding inside.

At the end of the summer, Laura lost her job at the Asia Society. HR explained it was due to restructuring, which made her feel okay until she learned no one else got laid off. She tried to figure out what she did wrong.

"Forget it," I said. "You didn't like the job that much anyway."

"But I did. I thought I was good at it. Didn't you think my articles were good?"

She bolstered herself, determined to spend the fall and winter enjoying unemployment and planning her next steps. But soon Laura had scrubbed the stove and microwave one time too many, and mopped the floors until her mop fell off its clamp. When she met up with friends and coworkers, they treaded lightly around work chatter and tried to assure her things happened for a reason.

I was working at Columbia as a research technician and going to graduate school for creative writing. At the time, Laura looked at me like I had it all figured out—I was on a path somewhere, like she had been, until recently. The problem wasn't that an attractive, well-educated, conscientious girl like Laura couldn't find a decent job—it was that she didn't know what she was good at anymore, and furthermore, she honestly didn't know what she wanted to do. She picked up *The Lover* and thought it was awful. She wondered out loud why it was fair things were working out for me. And still, how did I get someone as good-looking as Colin to sleep with me? Laura paced aimlessly. She'd slip on and off the couch. She resented me because she needed to talk and hated that I was the only one around; yet she would get angry at me for leaving her when we went out, for not coming to places when she invited me. But I was quietly falling apart on my own, and I just wanted to get away from her.

And where did I go? Those days, I always just ended up somewhere, and when the medication wore off, I'd realize it wasn't fun to find myself at a rounders set-up in a corporate building in Herald Square, or at the Pussycat Lounge, drinking from a liter in the men's bathroom with four anti-Palestine guys fresh out of the Israeli army, or nodding off at a bar, which I did often, answering random questions about myself.

I wondered what it was like to grow old in Queens. One afternoon, the lady from the apartment across from us rolled away on a gurney with a sheet over her head. The birdcage at her window was also covered with a black sheath. The next day, Animal Control came in with masks, black bags, and steel tanks. Her windows rattled like there was a storm inside. The morning I woke up in the snow, I went to a new psychologist who diagnosed me with bipolar mood disorder. The party ended when I could hardly get out of bed. When I'd wake up crying. When I'd contemplate shooting myself but couldn't gather the motivation to get up and buy a gun. It would take hours to find my keys. I ate only instant oatmeal for months. I was living in the Upper West Side, close to work. I was just functional enough not to get fired. My boss was a short, reformed Orthodox Jew who believed I had talent; I believed I had holes in my brain. By holes, I mean the black holes in people's souls that connect them to everyone else. When theoretical physics finally unlocks the secret to the universe, we'll see the subatomic thread that runs through each of us. I'd like to prove one day that we're all just dangling like fetuses on strings, floating in the density of dark gases.

I haven't spoken to Laura in five years. I left her soon after that winter. She'd completed her assignment at the magazine and had started graduate school in design and technology at Parsons. Her future was bright. But I left her because at parties and dinners, she'd greet me with happy eyes that reminded me of the pigeon lady and her glass of milk. It pained me that we were no longer close and pretending made me feel lonely at a time when I could barely keep track of the right pills. My new drug cocktail kept mania away but not depression. Laura couldn't understand what it felt like to stare into the Mekong River and accept that you'll be looking for the rest of your life; either she couldn't understand or she refused to look.

When I walk through Astoria, I find myself struck by familiar faces: old people worrying over stolen social security checks, worrying over who'd broken their angel fountains, and in the shadow of their worries lurks the end of young Laura and me. It's the saddest thing. Often I want to call her, but what would I say? Still I can't help but wonder if she ever thinks about the yellow afterglow of those summer afternoons, when we were hot and listless and we couldn't have known.

Chuckie

Victor LaValle

So it was me, my boys, and two new kids, Mark and Chuckie. All of us were heavy with equipment, the two new fellas with bikes. Saturdays parents existed only when we woke up and went to bed, the long line of hours in between were just baseball, baseball, baseball. We'd decided to stretch over to that park in the Italian neighborhood; the one near us was full.

The game went right: ground outs, pop flies, and stolen bases; I slid into second after a line drive and caught a nice piece of glass in my knee, it left the kind of scar you could roll up your jeans and brag about. While waiting to swing a bat we made up stories about girls far off we were fingering. We were almost ten and spoke loudly.

Baseball diamonds had been etched into the park, three separate plots. It was easy to find little ponds all over; like everything in Flushing they looked good from a distance. Only coming closer could you spy their murky gray insides. In the summers, very faintly, they emitted paint fumes. It was getting dark. That's how night arrived then, bothering you all at once, bursting into the room. One of us said, —Let's get the fuck out of here. We weren't Italian. Not even Mark. Not even Chuckie. This is not to say I had no Italian friends, our neighborhood was a mash of origins, but still, there were intricate politics. This was 1982. You knew where you could be and when.

We gathered up our mitts and balls and both aluminum bats Jung had carried on his wide shoulders. Half a block traveled and I had to run back for the left-handed glove Mom bought special after searching through six different Modell's for a first baseman's.

Then I chugged back to the guys on their feet, ahead of them Chuckie, Mark, and the bikes they'd rode in on, these dope silver Huffys. Those two had learned how to do spins, other tricks, and instantly I hated them like I did all my boys: secretly. Those ties didn't mean much to me. When you stopped speaking to some kid there would be another; one thing Flushing had in abundance was people.

Ahead, Mark was screaming. For us. Chuckie too. We got closer quickly. Beyond them all the setting sun's flames were running down to an orange gasp on the horizon. Two sweaty boys gripped one set of handlebars each. They were old enough to buy beer. Smiling and Laughing, that might as well have been their names. One said, —Come on, let us ride them once.

Mark said, —I gotta get home, man. He sounded like he was going to cry.

—Me and my friend just want to ride around the corner, said the other one. Smiling.

—We gotta help them, Jung pleaded. He had invited them along so what else could he say? We weren't fifteen feet off. The two thieves hadn't noticed us, didn't look even as we crossed the street: moving away. Chuckie and Mark were on their own.

The trees all around had been season-stripped of every leaf; pulsing winds made the branches crash and shake like hands applauding. Mark turned to us, then Chuckie, they took a moment to stare. Only the arms of the older duo moved as they tugged and jerked the bikes. We heard yelling. The chain-link fence surrounding an old home swayed loosely, its rattle a language. —Guys, Jung tried again. We should really go over and help.

—Will you shut the fuck up, I said. I was afraid the way people must be during a hurricane, thinking, Will it come for me? I had seen fights, started and lost them, I wasn't a novice. But this was a beating. Mark was thrown off his bike. Next Chuckie. Then the tall one was kicking Chuckie in the head. Mark got up and ran—not toward us, just away. I couldn't tell you how long those guys worked on Chuckie. It was a few minutes. Even one or two are very long. The blood started coming. I didn't know a face had so much. Helping was still an option for the others, but not me; it could have been Jung getting beat, my own father; many people would call me the betrayer, often, but that was because they'd mistaken me for a friend when I was just hanging around. There was only one kid I ever cared for and his name wasn't Chuckie. It wasn't any of these guys.

When a loud -pop- echoed from across the street I didn't flinch, wasn't even sure it had come from nearby.

Ten is too young to learn how you are. That you wouldn't run for the ambulance, as all my friends did, while Chuckie clutched at his eye like his very own soul was in danger of escaping. Booth Memorial didn't send an ambulance quickly. To the right, in the park, squirrels appeared, ruthlessly picking at the ground for food; from where I stood their quick little hops were even more graceful; when they ate energetically they seemed to be on their knees, paws forward in a frantic prayer.

Ethelerie's Blank Check

Arthur Nersesian

"Jamaica is a really, really dangerous neighborhood!" Paul warned. "It's always in the news. People are getting shot out there all the time." In truth, none of us knew shit about the place. Our choice was either to go out to Jamaica, Queens, where we were supposed to find some magical bus to take us all home, or stay homeless and hungry and wait for the crisis to pass.

The four of us were stuck out on Rockaway Beach. We hadn't eaten for twenty-four hours and things were starting to get desperate. In a scary *Lord of the Flies* fashion, my friend Paul confided to me and Ethelerie that he believed the whole mess was Isabelle's fault. She was my girlfriend back in the '90s. She got us all to go out for an afternoon trip at the beach yesterday and now we were stuck there. Perhaps this was what compelled her to come up with this half-baked plan. After a night of restless sleep on the beach, I was still dozing on the windy sand the next morning when Isabelle went out to search for a cup of coffee. That was when she crossed paths with one of the locals, setting this all in motion. I had been wearing my bathing suit for nearly twenty-four hours. Instead of the old flip-flops I had arrived in, I found a pair of hiking boots someone had abandoned on the boardwalk and pulled them on, making me look even more foolish. Together we all followed Isabelle to the stranger's house nearby. The older African American man lived just a block up from the beach. He was unloading stuff from the back of his old pickup truck, which was parked in his driveway. His rundown house had a big official-looking sign taped to the door that read *WARNING: Mold Contamination Detected.*

"You can't catch mold, can you?" Paul asked. I shrugged.

"Y'all ready?" the older man asked Isabelle, ignoring the three of us behind her.

"Yep," she spoke for us all.

He went inside the house. In the doorway we could see him trying to calm a tiny, older woman, presumably his wife, who seemed to be both sweating and shivering at once.

"What's the matter with her?" I asked Isabelle. The woman looked in bad shape.

"He said she needs insulin."

"Isn't there a hospital out here somewhere?"

"Yeah, but he said she's an outpatient at Jamaica Hospital, so . . ."

She had a tiny child's body and seemed as frail as glass. Paul offered to help, but the old fellow ignored all requests, assisting her alone into his old pickup truck.

"Is there anything that we can do?" Isabelle asked, never revealing how she met this guy or what we were supposed to do in exchange for the ride.

"Just don't rob me or the missus and you'll be fine," he said with a kindly smile.

"You hold up your end of the bargain, I'll hold up mine," she responded.

It was about one o'clock as we all tiredly piled into the back of his pickup and he started driving his clunker north, up the Rockaway Peninsula. Since he couldn't hear us, Paul asked Isabelle what exactly she was supposed to do in exchange for the drive. She explained that it was simple. She had met him while she was purchasing her coffee; he offered her a ride to the bus that went directly back to Manhattan. All we had to do was park his truck when he brought her into the hospital near the bus stop.

"Why didn't he just call an ambulance?" Ethelerie asked.

She shrugged. Even with health insurance, I knew that would cost a lot, and during this crisis they'd still probably have to wait for hours. This was definitely the best way to go. He sped around the jigsaw of streets and various housing projects, quickly getting us to the highway, which was a smart move as local streets were dangerous with the nonworking traffic lights.

Yesterday, August 14th, 2003, was a typical summer day. A sweltering hot Thursday. That morning Isabelle called and said she and her friend, Ethelerie, had had it with the heat. They were dashing out to the very edge of Queens and jumping into the ocean. Did I want to come?

"I'm way behind schedule." My latest novel had just gotten accepted by a publisher and it was one of those rare moments when someone was actually waiting for my work. But even with the air conditioner and the fan on, the heat was just sucking the focus out of me. "When are you going?"

"Right now. I'm meeting Ethelerie at the A train platform, on West Fourth Street in half an hour."

"See you there."

As soon as I clicked my cell phone, it rang back. It was my cousin Paul calling from where he lived down in Chinatown to complain about the heat. When I told him that I was dashing out to the Rockaways, he said he was coming, but had to leave early.

As we spoke, I pulled on my trunks and an old T-shirt, and slipped on a pair of wornout flip-flops. I also threw a towel and shorts into a small knapsack, along with a hundred pages of text to work on during the long train trip. I couldn't find my ATM card, so I grabbed ten bucks in loose dollars and a Metrocard with two swipes still on it.

About forty minutes later, I converged with Paul and the two gals on the subway platform. Paul brought his boogie board. Isabelle just brought herself. Perhaps, as a greeting gift, Ethelerie had bought a generous bag of healthy treats. Although we had both met her, we really didn't know her too well. Because my cousin was prone to panic attacks in the subway, we always had to board on the very front car. That way, if the train suddenly broke down mid-tunnel, the train operator could open the front door and just free poor Paul. To keep his twitchy mind off the claustrophobic conditions, he would manically toy with his iPod whenever he took the subway. As we headed into Brooklyn, people kept getting on. It wasn't until after Jay Street that passengers finally started exiting as we traversed Fort Greene and Bed Stuy. Throughout the subway car, among the usual drab commuters, I spotted a smattering of sharply dressed people, usually leaning on suitcases and knapsacks. They were the ones going out to JFK Airport. About halfway through the ride, after nearly forty-five minutes, when we finally were able to grab an angle of seats together, the train shot out of the tunnel, onto elevated tracks. After we reached Aqueduct Racetrack and then JFK Airport, most people got off and we found ourselves spreading out and chatting. Soon the train shot across the endless trestle over beautiful Jamaica Bay. By the time we reached Broad Channel, all others had gotten off, transferring to the S to head down the to the southern tip of Rockaway Peninsula. I convinced my group to save time by staying on the train. The next stop was Beach 67th Street. I had read that it was the most isolated station in all the

MTA's 660 miles of tracks. I remembered years ago, when my mother used to take me and my brothers out around here. Once the city decided that it wasn't fair that the rest of New York should have to pay for this extension of underused tracks; a second fare of ten cents was charged of Rockaway natives when they exited the trains.

Rows and rows of small bungalows made this area into a blue-collar Riviera during the hot weekend months when the city sizzled like it was in a deep-fry basket. Those bungalows had long ago been leveled and carted away. Since then the city had stuck rows of low income housing projects along the north stretch of the peninsula. Now this wonderful little stretch of New York, where the city ran right up against the Atlantic Ocean, had fallen into neglect. We walked through a solitary road that cut through the cleared field, straight to the new yet barren boardwalk, and across it to the stretch of neglected beach that was strewn with whatever garbage the ocean had washed up during the high tide.

Sometimes green-shirted youths, seasonal employees for the Parks Department, were stationed here, ordering bathers that they couldn't swim on the unguarded beach. That summer though, there seemed to be an employee shortage, so we took advantage by parking our towels on one empty beach north of the lifeguards and other sun worshippers. Lotion was quickly applied.

Cousin Paul took advantage of the relative desertion by stripping off his bathing suit and jumping naked into the rolling surf. Ethelerie, who was beautifully lean and olive-skinned, went topless. Only Isabelle and I, who had dated for roughly five years, remained fully suited. Usually Paul and I swam while Isabelle and Ethelerie chatted and worked on their tans; that day though, it was so hot, we all went in the water and stayed. The ocean was as warm as the Caribbean and as bouncy as an underage lover. Paul rode his boogie board again and again to ever-greater heights. For my part, I had always been an avid bodysurfer. Slowly, as always tends to happen, our happy group attracted others. Though there was ample space, newcomers meandering up the long boardwalk parked their towels and blankets on our little beach ever closer to us. Eventually my earth-boy cousin felt shamed into pulling back on his trunks and Ethelerie tied on her top.

About an hour and a half passed—a healthy stretch of time before, cooled down and exhausted, we stumbled back onto the warm sand. Ethelerie shared her bag of food: three avocados and four plump, juicy peaches. After gobbling down her generous gifts, Paul and I returned to the ocean, to more manic body and board surfing. It must've looked fun as the gals joined us a second time. The sheer pleasure made the time pass quickly. Paul was the first to point out that it was getting late. But the water was so invitingly warm and the city so brutally hot that we just couldn't bring ourselves to leave. In sheer exhaustion, Isabelle and Ethelerie finally collapsed on their towels while Paul and I just kept pushing ourselves, trying to squeeze the most out of our little excursion. Soon I saw Isabelle waving to us meekly, but in the heavenly levitation of warm waves, as though cradled in the arms of a loving and playful god, it was easy to ignore her.

When one particularly large black wave broke forth it propelled Paul and me all the way back to the reality of the shoreline. Isabelle greeted us with the news she had just learned from some passerby that the city was blacked out.

"What do you mean, 'blacked out?' " I asked, wiping off water that was running down my scalp.

"Some guy just said the whole city is out."

"What do you mean, 'out?' " Paul asked, hearing it only the second time.

"No electricity." she said.

"How about the subway?" Paul asked.

"It's *all* out," Isabelle said, struggling to get the message across.

"But it could come back on at any time," Ethelerie said, always hopeful.

We knew Paul suffered from claustrophobia in subway cars, but it turned out he was also fearful of serial killers when hitching rides from strangers. Twenty-four hours later, as we all sat in the hard metal bed of that stranger's pickup with the sickly lady in the shotgun seat, Paul first expressed concern that the stranger, who we thought was helping us, might be carting us all off to some desolate killing field. Vigilantly he warned us to look out for road signs and turn-offs, if only to confirm that we were vaguely heading toward the city. In the back of the truck though, the warm wind rushing through our hair made it difficult to talk. When we saw signs—first Edgemere and then one for Hewlett, where traffic started slowing down—he gradually felt more relaxed.

After nearly forty minutes, Isabelle smirked, pointing through the rear glass. The elderly woman in the front seemed to have gotten better, as she was swaying to some rock song coming over the radio, an amusing sight inasmuch as she was so old and frail. The driver suddenly swayed into the emergency lane and then he hit the gas. As we sped down the next exit ramp, he started honking his horn nonstop. Paul was the one who saw that the rocking woman had gone into full convulsions and we were all stuck in the back, unable to help them. As the old guy sped through lights, almost hitting pedestrians and drivers several times, people cursed at us stuck in the back. Finally, he screeched to a halt in front of Jamaica Hospital Medical Center, where he pushed open his door, raced around and grabbed his wife, who had fallen into the foot area of the truck. Paul jumped forward and helped him half carry, half drag the poor lady down the ER corridor, where they found a stray wheelchair and dropped her in. Then the old guy pushed her forth, trying to get her a shot of insulin.

While they were taking care of her, Isabelle declared, "I guess we're in Jamaica."

Cars behind us immediately started honking. The driver's door was still open with the engine running, so before we could get ticketed, Isabelle and I got in the front seat, which was loaded with garbage. Paul suddenly returned and jumped in the back with Ethelerie. We drove down Jamaica Avenue, all of us looking for a parking spot. Finally, after a few blocks, we saw some guy pulling out from a meter, in front of what looked like a city park. Isabelle made a wild U-turn and backed into the spot. We were all impressed by how well she drove a truck. She rolled up the windows and locked the doors but when she tried to remove the keys, she was unable. It took about ten minutes to figure out that she had to turn the steering wheel until it locked, and only then could we remove the key.

"What now?"

"Oh," Paul said. "He told me to park the truck and bring him back the key."

"Where exactly are we parked?" Isabelle asked. Paul discovered that the name of the park was Martin Luther King Park, so we headed back down Jamaica Avenue to give the man his keys and tell him.

After another five minutes or so, the four of us wearily marched back to the hospital. Isabelle and I went into the Emergency Room while Paul and Ethelerie waited outside. The first thing I noticed was the fact that the lights and air conditioning were on; emergency generators were working full-time in the hospital. In the waiting area, all the chairs were packed with sickly people. Standing in a corner and staring out a window was the old guy. I stood off to one side while Isabelle approached. She politely returned his key and told him where she had parked his truck.

"This whole thing," he said, tensely. "What a goddamn mess!"

"Did you have some medicine in the fridge or something . . . ?"

"It had nothing to do with the blackout. She takes pills. I just thought we had some left."

"Is she okay?"

"I don't know. The convulsions were bad."

I made a gesture to go; we still had no idea of how to get back home. Isabelle told him where his truck was parked and thanked him again. Outside, we were surprised to see Paul hugging Ethelerie. They quickly broke up when we approached.

"All right," Paul spoke up first. "We talked about it and decided that we can't go any further without food."

Without his seeing it, Ethelerie shrugged, suggesting they hadn't said a word.

"There's a city bus around here somewhere that'll get us back to the city," Isabelle said. "Why don't we find it first and . . ."

"We're hours away from Manhattan, even on a good day," Paul replied. "Even if we find this bus soon, with all this traffic, who knows how long it'll be before we get home?"

"And I have to use a bathroom," Ethelerie said.

"All right." I tried to bring everything together. "Let's find some food, a bathroom, and then this fucking bus."

"How much money do we got?" Isabelle asked. We pooled all our cash. We barely had thirty dollars. All but me had brought their ATM cards, which were useless during the blackout.

"Oh wait," Ethelerie said suddenly. "I have a blank check!"

"Do you have ID?" Paul asked.

"Yes, but . . ." She carefully went through her pockets but couldn't find her wallet; she always carried a small wallet on her.

"Shit, I left my wallet in the back of the truck."

"Are you sure?" I asked.

"I was sitting there for the past hour. If it's not there . . ." With that she seemed to panic and started running down Jamaica Avenue. Paul was in close pursuit and Isabelle and I followed, back to the city park where the car was parked, about five blocks south.

"Do you think there's any chance that Paul and Ethelerie slept together?" Isabelle asked softly.

"No way, why?"

"I thought I heard—I don't know . . . synchronized breathing last night."

"He would've told me," I said, and wondered if they had slept together.

Roughly five minutes later, we watched as Ethelerie jumped into the back of the pickup and found her wallet. Opening it up, she took out the check and waved it in the air.

"My god, I can't believe no one stole your wallet. And in this neighborhood! I was just sitting there," Paul said.

"What do you mean, 'this neighborhood?' " Ethelerie asked.

"I'm sure he just meant New York City," I said.

"So this is what we'll do," Paul resumed, pointing behind us, up toward Sutphin Boulevard. "Let's go up to that avenue, which seems to be the busiest. And we'll check out all the restaurants and try to find a good one. Then we'll go in and see if they'll take her check and if they don't, we'll try a second one, and we'll just keep doing that until we find a place that does."

"Hey," Ethelerie said, pointing to a sign. "It's not Martin Luther King Park. It's Rufus King Park."

"Who said it was Martin Luther King?" Isabelle asked. Was it racist to assume that a city park called King in an African American neighborhood would be named after the martyred civil rights leader?

"Who the hell's Rufus King?" I asked, reading the sign. It turned out he was an interesting historical figure. In addition to being one of New York's first senators, he was against slavery and was a major politician of his day.

"And he lived in a black neighborhood before it was cool," Paul pointed out, but we all knew he was kidding. Back then, all this had to be farmland.

When we reached Sutphin, we found the boulevard was lined with restaurants. Going from place to place, we checked out the menus posted in the windows on both sides of the street. Quickly we narrowed it down to two choices, almost directly across the street from each other. One was Mohammed Halal Pakistani Restaurant, which looked like an army mess hall for cabbies. It had rows of tables. Along the rear were rows of steamer trays, piled high with brown, dark yellow, and darker green foods swimming in sauces, as well as a mountain of white rice. According to the large red sign in the window, for eight bucks you could grab a porcelain plate and eat to your heart's content—something Paul and I found exquisitely alluring. The alternative was a small hole-in-the-wall place directly across Sutphin called Golden Krust Caribbean Bakery & Grill.

"You don't understand; 'Halal' means *all you can eat!*" Paul said, as if they had missed it.

"No, it doesn't," I said, "but they do have an all you can eat deal."

"But this is Jamaica, Queens," Isabelle countered, pointing to the Caribbean place, "and that's a Jamaican restaurant!"

"Screw that!" I retorted. "We haven't eaten in twenty-four hours. And we can eat nonstop over there."

"You're just looking to fill your gullets!"

"That's true, but it's not like either of these places are ever going to be featured on the Food Network. I mean, we're starving," Paul said innocently.

"You guys want to eat in that men's room," Isabelle lashed out, "be my guest; I'll wait until I get back to the city." Somehow it had become a battle of the sexes.

"You're just against it 'cause they're Arabic," I continued, in the same vein of humor.

"It's Ethelerie's check. How about we let her decide?" Paul said, making me wonder if Isabelle was right about the two of them.

"Okay," Isabelle said, turning to her. "Where do you want to eat?"

"Well, we *are* in Jamaica, Queens," she said simply and that was it.

Paul and I let out a sigh and the four of us crossed the street. We still had reason to hope that they would refuse Ethelerie's check so we could gorge ourselves on endless plates of greasy male food. Despite the blackout, which robbed it of possible reggae music and air conditioning, the Caribbean diner had no atmosphere. There were seven equidistant tables that looked like they had been robbed from McDonald's and no pictures on the walls. Though the place was packed, we were the only whites there.

We got in line and looked at the menu board on the far wall. Under "Reggaefeast Combos" they included callaloo and salt fish, curry goat, oxtail stew, jerk chicken, and curry shrimp meal. All lunches were priced between eight and ten bucks.

"We have a bit of a problem," Ethelerie said timidly to one of the two clerks on duty. "We went out to Rockaway Beach yesterday when the lights went out . . ."

"We had to sleep right on the beach last night," Isabelle joined in earnestly.

"And now we're a little low on cash . . ." Ethelerie resumed.

"We don't give charity," said the older of the two cashiers firmly.

"No, we have a check," Ethelerie said holding up the check. "We just don't have credit cards or cash."

"Do you have some photo ID?" the woman asked.

"Yeah." Ethelerie held up her New York State license.

"I don't normally do this," she said with a Caribbean accent, "but seeing as how the city is out and the food's going bad, I'll make an exception for you."

Paul and I both breathed a sigh or relief. Though we wanted the all-you-can-eat deal across the street, we knew they could just as easily have refused a check, and a meal in the hand was better than two in the halal buffet. Isabelle suggested mixing and matching, so we ended up getting two orders of jerk chicken, a curry goat, and an oxtail stew. They all came with rice and peas, fried plantains, and a heated bread called roti. Ethelerie signed her check and included a generous gratuity—forty bucks. Over the course of the next fifteen minutes, as other orders were bagged and delivered, we waited for a table. When one group of Rasta-looking types rose to leave, Paul tossed his boogie board on their table. Ethelerie wiped it down while Isabelle poured four cups of warm water from an available pitcher in the corner. Soon our order came out. Though the meals didn't earn any points for presentation, the food was bursting from the plates and the flavors were memorable. The fusion of Indian, Caribbean, and European was an exquisite balancing act of continents and cultures. As we swapped food, I was happy to find that the spicy flavor of the curry goat was unlike the nuttier taste of the jerk chicken. Certainly it had something to do with the fact that none of us had really had consumed more than Ethelerie's food in the past day, but it was still a wonderful meal, almost worth the wait. The oxtail stew tasted fresh, as if it had just been clipped from the rear of the poor animal. Though it might've been fattening, it was so richly authentic that I couldn't remember the last time I'd had something so tasty.

In fact, Isabelle started coaching Paul and me to intermittently put down our forks between bites, as we were scarfing down our food at a faster pace than she and Ethelerie. The whole meal did seem to pass far too quickly. Once we finished, we used our unleavened roti bread to wipe down our plastic plates, leaving them shiny with grease. Only then did we clean off the table after us and thank the woman who trusted Ethelerie's check. Isabelle politely inquired if she knew where we could catch the bus back to Manhattan.

"Oh yeah, the Q60 up on Archer," she said, pointing to the right. "It's on the corner."

"Pardon me," Paul said her before we left the establishment. "Did they name this neighborhood after Jamaicans moved here or . . . ?" I tensed up, fearing he'd accidentally say something offensive.

"No, that's what everyone thinks," she said with her Marley-esque accent. "The name of this place is actually corruption of a native Indian word for 'beaver.' "

"You're kidding," Ethelerie replied, slightly embarrassed. It seemed to undermine her reason for selecting the restaurant.

"I read about it on Wikipedia," said the clerk.

Before walking out, Paul asked where the bathroom was, which reminded the rest of us to do the same. Since there were two small toilets in the back, we let the women use them first. While alone, I asked Paul if he had sex with Ethelerie last night.

"God, no!" he replied with a chuckle. "I mean, I would, but she'd never sleep with me. Why would you even ask that?"

"Why were you hugging when we left the hospital?"

"Oh, she said the old guy reminded her of her grandfather who she only saw a few times in her life."

"You're kidding!"

"Why would I be kidding?" he asked.

"I didn't know she was black," I said, not that anything was wrong with that. "Is Ethelerie a black name?"

"It's just a name."

Soon the two women were done so Paul and I went to the bathrooms next. When we were finished, we thanked the clerk again and left. As we walked up Sutphin, a young African American man muttered something as we passed. A few steps later, another guy surreptitiously muttered some one-word phrase.

"What are they peddling?" Ethelerie asked.

"Not sure," Paul replied.

At the corner up ahead we saw elevated tracks going into a huge multilevel complex with a broad, spectral stainless-steel awning shooting out front. As we got closer to the corner, we could see big shiny letters bolted to the side of an older building that said LIRR.

A moment later we passed another African American man and all clearly heard him say, "Taxi?"

"They must work picking up people from the LIRR station."

"Oh, and they're not licensed," Ethelerie deduced. "That's probably why they're selling it like pot."

"Do you know where the bus back to the city is?" Isabelle asked the taxi peddler.

"Right there," he pointed a half a block down. A large empty bus was barreling toward us. "But you better hurry. It turns at the corner!"

As we sprinted up the block, we thought, we were going to have the entire bus to ourselves. But when we reached the corner of Archer Street, the bus turned before a massive line and went about ten feet beyond it. When its front door opened, the line broke into pandemonium and everyone mobbed around it. In a rare moment of cunning, Paul led us to the back door, which was closer to us. He jammed his fingers past the rubber door guard and managed to trigger the automatic pole; it popped open. Using his boogie board as a kind of shield, we raced up the aisle, still in our bathing suits, and desperately rushed into two rows of double seats. We were safely behind the priority seating rows so at very least, wherever this bus finally terminated, we had seats for the duration. That alone made us feel a moment of joy. And, of course, the air conditioner felt great. But the bus wasn't going anywhere fast. It took another five interminable minutes, until the vehicle was filled to bone-crunching capacity, before the front door finally folded shut. During that time, we realized we had no idea of the bus's final destination. Just as she had sworn about the existence of this magic bus, Isabelle, with keen intuition, now swore it was the right one.

It was around two o'clock when that crowded conveyance, like a third-class train from Calcutta, rolled forth. None of us really knew Queens, so when we saw a street sign that said 139th Street and 91st Avenue, it sounded like an intersection somewhere in Ohio. Soon we passed houses with front porches and gated front yards. With a smirk, Paul silently pointed out the Gifted Minds Academy for Children. I smiled. When we circled around, we drove right past Jamaica Hospital. Looking at the sign, I realized the narrow, barren two-way street we had crossed was none other than the nascent beginnings of mighty Queens Boulevard.

"Oh, god!" Ethelerie yelled, and pointing behind her she said, "Look!"

We all turned, but the bus moved so quickly, none of us caught anything.

"What did you see?"

"We got to get off!" she said, rising from her seat. The bus came to a stop and the light on the back door opened.

"What are you talking about?" Paul said, grabbing her.

"He was crying on the street!" she said as she pulled away.

"Who?"

"The old guy. We have to help him! Let go of me!" She rose and pushed her way to the back door.

"Are you nuts?" Isabelle asked.

"His wife died!" Ethelerie said. "He shouldn't be alone like that." Before she could exit, the bus resumed moving. She shoved on the pole, yelling for the driver to stop.

Paul handed me his boogie board as he rose, losing his seat. He went over to her and said, "You don't know that she died. You just know you feel bad, but we did whatever we could for him. Believe me, even if she did die, he won't want us to bother him."

Slightly embarrassed, Ethelerie nodded silently. With both of their seats now occupied, they stood in the back of the bus. Over the next four hours, as the blackout continued, Isabelle and I took turns letting them sit in our seats. Our packed bus slowly made its way across Queens, finally crossing the 59th Street Bridge, back to Manhattan.

The Maspeth Holders

Margarita Shalina

Jhessika woke me at six in the morning with a cup of sweet milky coffee. She gingerly hopped up onto the bed, navigating her way between sleeping cat torsos. "Come on, it's time to get up," she said. In one hour, the Maspeth Holders were going to be demolished.

It had been on the local news and in the papers that week. Jhess had come home from work the previous night and plopped onto her velvety, vintage-circa-1970-something, big-papa den chair, purchased from the large antique shop run out of a garage on Metropolitan Avenue, just before Mt. Olivet cemetery. A suit of armor shimmered in the sun during store hours, standing sentinel and strange out front on the sidewalk. Opening the newspaper, she'd said, "The gas tanks on Maspeth Avenue are going to be demolished tomorrow. We're going."

"I can't; I have to work tomorrow. Take Holly or Jeanie."

"No, it's Sunday. You don't start work until a quarter to eleven. The gas tanks are coming down at seven. I'll get you up." Then she added in a sing-song manner, "I'll make coffee."

"They're blowing them up? You want to see shit get blown up?" I asked.

"Yes!" she replied, grinning. She lit incense, put on one of her woeful jazz diva CDs, and began rolling a joint. I watched her against the backdrop of the soft mauve walls from my place on the futon where I sat, cross-legged. She lit the joint and inhaled, then passed it over and summarized the article from the paper, reading chunks aloud. "The natural division and logistical border between Queens and Brooklyn is Newtown Creek. The tanks are visible from every point in the industrial park, which occupies both Greenpoint in Brooklyn and West Maspeth in

Queens. On Sunday, July 15, 2001, the four hundred-foot tall Maspeth Holders, also known as the Brooklyn Union Gas Tanks, located on the Brooklyn side of Newtown Creek on Maspeth Avenue in Greenpoint, are scheduled to be demolished at 7:00 a.m. The first tank was constructed in 1927. The second, constructed in 1948, serves as a marker light for LaGuardia Airport."

"That sounds excellent!" I agreed, inhaling and passing the joint back. Jhess got up and walked out the front door to retrieve her mountain bike from the tiny hallway that fell away abruptly to a crooked set of stairs. She went out to do reconnaissance work, scouting locations from where we could best see the destruction.

The minute I stepped into the hall, I realized our landlord, Aslan, was hammering away at Beata's apartment on the first floor. Paranoia set in. I quietly closed the door and retreated to the mauve bedroom where incense burned, masking our indiscretion. Beata's bathroom had a leak—a legendary, reoccurring, almighty leak that ate drywall and devoured plaster like a mid-twentieth-century army fueled by a belief in National Socialism. Aslan, like many small-time landlords in New York, was terrified of the leak being exactly what it was: a plumbing problem. Insisting he was a certified plumber himself, he kept drywalling Beata's bathroom ceiling. Every four to six months, the drywall would melt away from water damage. Each time we showered upstairs, it rained in her bathroom downstairs.

Aslan was Albanian and married with a brood of what seemed like countless adolescent girls. He had a brusque but pleasant manner and an intense birthmark on his face that resembled a fake beauty spot found in trashy period movies depicting the court of Louis XIV. A contractor by trade, he lived on Staten Island. He'd bought and fixed up the Maspeth house, then rented out the two units, plus a small stand-alone house in back that bordered where the ground fell away to railroad tracks. Freight trains ran on those tracks once or twice a day and the whole house shook.

His wife was a colossus named Sultana, a hulking woman made even larger by her penchant for stiletto heels. She liked leather miniskirts, tight tops, and shearlings. She had the midsection of a woman who'd birthed a litter. Her bleached, pin-straight hair did nothing but accentuate her tawdry fashion sense. I imagined that she didn't have breasts so much as vertical rows of teats. She spoke so loudly, I wondered if she wasn't mildly deaf. I called her "Slut-Anna" behind her back. Whenever the rent went up, Aslan would send Slut-Anna to announce it like a medieval herald. She was incapable of subtly handing over the lease while saying, "The rent increase is noted." Instead, she'd come upstairs, hands on birthing hips, place one thick thigh ending in a black stiletto boot across our threshold, and say in her screechy voice full of embittered venom, "From now on"—drum roll please—"rent is . . ." Place a cymbal crash after the dollar sign!

No one comes to Maspeth by accident. Even my mother planned weeks in advance to make the trek from Manhattan's Lower East Side. We threw parties over the years and invariably ended up running a mini motel for stragglers who were intimidated by the commute home. Everyone was welcome to the couch. We are 60-35 62nd Avenue, between 60th Street and 60th Place—not an uncommon address for Queens, which was once farmland and seems to have no cohesive urban planning behind its overall design. It's easier to say that we're just off of Metropolitan Avenue where it intersects with Eliot, right before Fresh Pond Road, after the Jewish cemetery but before the Episcopalian. Having never worked outside of Manhattan, I commuted from Queens the entire eight years that I lived in Maspeth. I'd take the Q54 through the industrial park to Metropolitan and Grand, then the L train into the city. I grew up on the Lower East Side and I never learned to drive.

Every workday morning began with the Q54, a ridiculously long bus route starting somewhere in Jamaica and ending at a depot by the foot of the Williamsburg Bridge. With such a long route, bunching occurred often; two or three buses showed up at once, then nothing for twenty minutes to a half hour. The posted schedules weren't realistic. Our neighborhood was off the grid while being on the map and the commute was tough and exhausting. I saw the same people each morning at the bus stop, though we never spoke. We crossed Newtown Creek together—really English Kills, the creek's little dead-end waterway vein—and we held our breath as one. The water was carcinogenic.

Buses ran erratically and the drivers were burned-out and ruthless. This past Saturday morning, I'd found myself begging for mercy. The bus was idling at the stop, its doors closed, the driver waiting for the light to change. I pleaded with the civil servant to open the door, tapping and calling, "Excuse me! Excuse me, sir! Sir, you're still at the stop!" After a protracted minute, he took off, showering me in exhaust. I'd be late to work again. I prepared myself to release a litany of profanity pertaining to the womb that brought him into this world, when an SUV pulled up before me, braking hard on Metropolitan and Forest.

A woman leaned over the passenger side and yelled, "I saw the whole thing. Get in!" High on adrenaline, I jumped in, not thinking twice.

"Are we gonna catch him?" I asked, laughing.

"Yeah! Right! I saw what he did. That was just rude!" she shouted back.

An uneasy silence quickly settled in around us. We realized, looking sideways at one another, that perhaps we had been rash, both of us now mutually nervous. Immediately anxious to be rid of me, she asked, "So, where are you going?" Immediately anxious to be out of the car, I recalled the closing scene of *Foxes* in flashes: pouty, pink-lipped Cherie Currie dying in a car crash after being picked up by a creepy swinger couple. I glanced at the backseat.

"I'm going to the L, on Grand and Metropolitan."

"Great." She sighed in relief and smiled.

"Great," I echoed. We drove along Metropolitan, cheering as we passed the bus at a stop in the industrial park.

Maspeth consists of warehouses, factories, Western Beef Supermarket, New Penn Trucking, Asian Import/Exporters, gas stations advertising diesel, garages, the surprise of nearly forgotten train tracks that still transport freight, junkyard cemeteries encapsulating the vestiges of dead cars, junkyard dogs roaring unexpectedly at fences. It's the workplace of men and women who perform physically demanding labor and retire with back problems and painkiller addictions. A place where black P.O.W./M.I.A. flags still hang proudly below the promise of, "You are not forgotten." The workplace of men and women on work release—convicts. The workplace of newly arrived immigrants with limited skill sets, who have yet to achieve fluency in English. The workplace of labor on the night shift. A neighborhood of strip bars with names like *Pumps* or *The Treasure Chest*. Everyone who works here punches a time clock. The region is glutted with traffic, illuminated nocturnally by the headlights of massive eighteen-wheel trucks delivering cargo, skids of freight, as truckers stick their heads out of behemoth vehicles, surveying the lower stratum.

"Five more minutes," I moaned to Jhess, over the repetitive groan of the antiquated air-conditioning unit in the bedroom window. I had a gnawing fear that one day my relic of an air conditioner would go flying from its perch in the window of our aluminum-sided home and crush some small Polish child below. This fear wasn't completely groundless; there was no shortage of Polish children and the infrastructure of our building was less than perfect.

Our downstairs neighbors were Zygmunt and Beata. Damion was their son. He lived up to the legacy of what I'd decided was his namesake, the demon seed from *The Omen*. It wasn't his fault; his father beat his mother. He had an unusually raspy voice for a child and, like his parents, was still in the process of learning English. At night, his little raspy voice would become a scream: "MAMA! MAMA! No! Don't hurt Mama! Leave Mama alone!" Then the sound of furniture crashing, any tchotchke at Zygmunt's arms' length made airborne, then broken. The dull, thumping sounds of an open hand making contact with flesh repeatedly. A body smashing against a wall. Beata, a slender five foot four brunette with bright blue eyes—a beautiful woman and noticeably younger than Zygmunt—could often be seen with sunglasses on, her pretty face discolored and bruised. You could tell they'd met in Poland before emigrating to the States. You could tell that he'd promised her a different life from the one they were living.

As Zygmunt unraveled and dove further into his pathetic, belligerent drinking, turning into a fat, slobbering mess, the more visibly unhappy Beata became and the more uncontrollable Damion was. At times, she'd make the walk upstairs to our door, humiliated, her little white robe torn and her face bruised and swelling, and ask us to call the police; Zygmunt had ripped their phone out of the wall. At first I'd snickered about her name—"Dude, she's a beaten wife named Beata," I'd mock. Jhess would laugh and shake her head.

Beata and I didn't get along. She was in her twenties like us, maybe a bit older. At our worst, she'd scream "crazy Russian" and I'd retort with "stupid Pole." Eventually, the name-calling ceased and we began going downstairs to knock on the door, unprompted, when we heard Zygmunt beating Beata. The noise would stop abruptly. Jhess, using her authoritative butch voice, would call out, "Beata, are you alright? Do you need help? Do you want us to call the police?"

Zygmunt kept coming home drunk. He'd stopped driving and was constantly dropped off at the house no earlier than midnight by a rowdy bunch crammed into an automobile, yelling, "Good night, Ziggy! Bye, Ziggy!" He'd stumble to the front door, waving and laughing. "Oh-kay. Bye, guys!" It was almost endearing.

He'd fumble with his keys, slam the front door as loudly as possible, stumble over the threshold and jostle his apartment door. Beata had begun waiting up for him, antagonizing him about the company he was keeping. She'd recently switched from yelling in Polish to yelling in accented English, just to make sure the whole block was on the same page.

"O—you were with your boy-friend?!"

Smack!

"Getting drunk with your boy-friend again?!"

Smack!

"You love him so much—why don't you fuck him?"

As she stood at our door, bleeding and swelling, Jhessika looked at her and said, "You can't keep doing this. We'll help you however we can but you can't keep living like this. He's abusing you. He doesn't have the right to hurt you. You deserve respect. You deserve someone who'll love you. If you don't do it for yourself, think about your little boy." She looked up at us, then quickly averted her eyes like a scolded schoolgirl.

"He's teaching Damion what kind of man to become," I added sheepishly, aware that Beata hated me. We may not have acknowledged them, but we didn't have any secrets in the house; our proximity to one another prevented it. "Look, we've been living here together for years, Beata, and it's not getting any better. You know that. He's an abuser, nothing but a wife beater."

Earlier in the year, Beata finally called the police and had drunken Zygmunt taken away in what resembled a paddy wagon, as the cops mercilessly mocked and teased him. Ranting and raving, he was falling over attempting to explain what the problem was in broken, accented *mano-a-mano* speak.

"Look . . ." he relayed. "She's a bee-tch. She's got boy-frrr-end. He fa-a-a-t and au-gly!"

When we finally did get a look at Beata's new boyfriend, we saw a mild-mannered, six-foot-tall, blond-haired, blue-eyed Polish man in his late twenties with a casual summer tan. He had remarkably broad shoulders and muscular arms and he resembled an illustration from a Soviet propaganda poster, depicting the ideal Slavic man. Even little Damion looked up at him meekly, shy and in awe, his little raspy voice all warm butter.

The night Zygmunt was ousted, all of Maspeth heard Beata screaming at the top of her lungs, her r's rolling wild and not one single article dropped. *"You are abusing me! You don't have the r-r-right! I deserve r-r-respect! You are damaging my son! Abus-er-r-r! Wife beat-er-r-r-r!"*

Jhess walked into the bedroom. Its windows faced out onto the street. "Oh, God," she sighed. "What now?"

"No! You have to hear this," I quickly said.

We pulled up the blind and opened the window as far as it would go, leaning out to embolden her with our presence. Our Beata had triumphed.

I extended my arm and groped for my eyeglasses as Jhess sat watching patiently. I found the coffee mug and sipped. Sat up. Sipped. Scooped up the limp and lazy cat torso to my left with one hand and dragged it across my lap, leaving it at rest against the wall. I sipped again, put down the coffee and stumbled, cursing and clumsy, to the bathroom, where I pulled my waist-length hair back into a bun and looked in the mirror. I hadn't had my hair professionally cut in eleven years. It wasn't bad, but I did appear as though I'd been living in the mountains for the past decade, washing it in a stream with a brick of lard soap. I treated my hair as though it had nerve endings. I took my meds.

"Okay, let's go," I said, when I was fully dressed.

"Yay!" Jhess clapped encouragingly, like a little girl. "Got the keys!" she called out, grabbing them from the table that stood opposite the front door.

On the street, I turned instinctively toward Metropolitan Avenue, where the Q54 ran. "No, no. We're going this way," Jhess said, leading me to the right, toward Maspeth proper.

"Aren't we going to the industrial park?" I asked. She responded in the affirmative but led me toward Flushing Avenue.

We boarded an unfamiliar bus line and swiped our Metrocards, then got off after ten minutes. We were in the industrial park but at a perspective that I was unaccustomed to. It was bleakly beautiful. Miniscule concrete and rubble debris berries rested on the sidewalks and streets like fat pollen released from birch trees in summer. Carcinogenic Newtown Creek reeked close by but was not visible. We walked down streets that were deceptively deserted; I knew it was just industry abandoned in the off hours, like the canyons of Wall Street on weekends. The sun shone brightly on large squares of pavement penetrated by weeds. The architecture reminded me of a postapocalyptic movie, the warehouses harboring sleeping zombies that rose with moonlight. We wove in and out of alleys, stepped over train tracks.

"Watch the glass!" she said, mindful of my aversion to regular shoes.

"Yeah! I know!" I responded, annoyed yet nervous that my pretty flip-flops might be unexpectedly pierced by some shard of compressed sand. The air smelled of morning.

We began to see other people around us, heading this way and that, seeking a good view. We emerged from the labyrinth to a concrete courtyard peppered by weeds. "No, this isn't it," Jhess said, checking her watch. We turned again, making our way through more low-rise factories and seemingly dilapidated but functional buildings in shades of brown and gray. We took large strides over concrete barriers meant for vehicles and entered onto yet another courtyard peppered with weeds. A tree, seemingly out of place, was making an attempt at life through the concrete. I looked up at the Maspeth Holders: tall, cylindrical, and lovely.

"I've never seen them from this angle before," I said, beginning to grow excited. As we entered the courtyard, there were others there already. Quiet people, solemn in their own expectations, were focused on the structures, some with cameras or camcorders and some, like us, with only their memories at the ready.

"We're here!" Jhess said. The Holders stood before us, their red and white picnic-tablecloth crowns towering just above.

"When?" I asked.

"Soon," she answered. It was 6:45 a.m. We were fifteen minutes early. I looked over at her pretty face in the morning light.

"So this is the best we can do for entertainment in Maspeth, huh?" I joked, looking to my left at the Manhattan skyline. It was early. I looked at the people around us. I imagined our industrial park was made of green grass and that we had all brought picnic blankets and brunches, bottles of wine. My eyes fell back on the Holders.

"Now," she said. "It should be now."

We didn't move. We didn't breathe. We watched the tall and steely grey twins, transfixed. We gasped.

Light travels faster than sound. When the explosives detonated, we saw a Christmas tree formation of lights. They lit up abruptly, all around the barrel bellies of the Holders; a second later, the sound of explosives rang out from both structures. They hesitated before falling, as though they'd both hopped into the air for an instant; then the collapse ensued. They buckled, one then the other. I heard gasps all around us as the buildings fell into an abyss of their own debris and destruction. The aftermath, clouds of gray ash and smoke, was localized—safe, elsewhere. A shock of birds scattered, disturbed, horrified, bursting into the morning sky. We—all transfixed. I brought my hands together, as though I were on a plane that had just touched down on the tarmac safely, despite challenging weather conditions. The reverb came at me from behind. We—all applauding. We—all reverential.

The phone was ringing, ringing, ringing . . . the sound like a siren. "A-ll-o?" I mumbled into the receiver, scrambling through the sheets and cat bellies on the futon. It was chilly in the room; Jhess turned the air conditioner off when she'd gotten up for work. The weather was changing. *What a beautiful morning*, I momentarily thought, squinting up at the sun-drenched bedroom.

"Margarita, GET UP!"

"I'm up, why are you yelling at me?" I moaned.

"Get Jeanie up. Turn the TV on, NOW! Don't go to work. I'll be home as soon as I can."

"What the fuck are you talking about?" I grumbled, looking at the clock. It was about ten minutes to 9:00 a.m.

"A plane went into the World Trade Center."

Jhess had been working as a security guard for the past three months at a mail-processing company that had recently relocated from Middle Village to one of the enormous warehouse spaces of the Brooklyn Navy

Yard. The company employed people down on their luck—people without degrees, high school or otherwise, single mothers, men and women on work-release, recovering drug addicts. I imagined them all crowded around large industrial windows, the mothers quieter than the rest as thoughts of retrieving their children from other neighborhoods, other boroughs, began to stir in their conscious minds.

"Jhess?"

"Just don't go anywhere! And make sure Jean doesn't either."

"She's stay-cationing." I mumbled. "I don't understand. Jhess, will Holly be alright? The Alfred Smith projects are right there." Holly, Jhessika's best friend, had been earning her MSW while working as a welfare-to-workfare counselor in lower Manhattan.

"Holly will probably show up at the apartment. Stay where you are. I love you. I have to go."

"Jhess?"

She hung up.

I jumped out of bed and turned on the TV, threw open my bedroom door and ran to Jeanie's bedroom, banging open-palmed on her door.

"Jean! Jean-ie! Get up! JEANIE! NOW!"

I ran back to my room and soon Jeanie came lumbering in, rubbing her eyes. One of the World Trade Center towers was smoldering on the TV screen.

"What happened?" Jeanie asked.

"That," I said, pointing helplessly.

I grew up in the apartment where my mother has lived since 1981 and I attended P.S. 134 on Grand Street. Our class trips included visits to the World Trade Center observation deck, where small, inner-city urchins ran about like feral cats with brown-bag lunches. They would occasionally stop to press palms and foreheads against the tall glass windows, only to recoil, overwhelmed by fear and vertigo as the building noticeably swayed to and fro. As we grew and ventured out of our neighborhood, the Twin Towers became a compass needle tip, signifying south. We are a generation that grew up in the shadow of the World Trade Center.

When the second plane penetrated the South Tower, Jeanie began to cry. I felt anxious.

"Do you want coffee?" I asked, walking into the kitchen. We were out of sugar. I felt the overwhelming need to be out on the street. "Jean, I'm going for sugar. I'll be right back."

Sirens screamed nearby, then faded into the distance. *They're calling in all responders*, I realized. I turned right and walked down 62nd Street, passing Mike, a scrappy German shepherd belonging to the mechanics at the corner. He had a gracious habit of stopping as I passed in the mornings, as though tipping his hat.

As I stepped onto Metropolitan Avenue, the horizon unfurled like a panoramic cityscape painting before me. Maspeth was the first European settlement in Queens, probably because the southernmost part of Maspeth, where I lived, is the borough's highest point. Gray smoke billowed from lower Manhattan. The city was wounded. The firmament appeared one shade darker than powder blue, crystalline and devoid of white cotton-candy clouds, marred by something like car exhaust. The towers burned, a conflagration whose smoke rose ever higher. A spectacle in the clear, sunny September blight. Our crepuscular millennial fireworks of char wove serpentine through air, disseminating to gray haze. North seemed untouched; the Empire State building resembled a neighbor watching another neighbor's house on fire. The distant sirens became tolling bells. I thought of my grandmother surviving the Blockade and wondered if this was what war felt like. I thought of destruction. I thought of the Maspeth Holders.

Our neighborhood, which most people can't find on a map, lost nineteen first responders that day. They were from two units that shared a fire house at 56-29 68th Street; eight were firefighters from Squad 288 and eleven were from Hazmat 1. Hazardous Materials 1 is the most specialized unit in all of New York City. Their motto: *Fortuna Favet Fortibus*, "Fortune favors the strong."

A local firehouse on Metropolitan came into view. All the fire trucks had gone. Sirens could be heard blaring all around, bound for Manhattan. Firefighters were still trickling in. Entering the house, they shook hands and smiled at one another in a way I found disturbing.

I entered the Fire House Deli, where I'd been purchasing my bad coffee loyally for years. The deli had changed many hands but was now owned and run by a Korean couple who had one employee to work the deli counter. I walked in unnoticed. The Korean wife and the Mexican employee were watching the towers burn on television. I stood with them, transfixed, until they both looked over, shaking their heads and smiling sadly. Neither of them spoke English especially well and I wondered how they understood one another's radically different accents.

The Korean wife shook her head. "Terrible," she said, her R-sound bleeding into an L-sound.

"Terrible." The Mexican deli guy nodded, his R-sound rolling Spanish.

"Terrible," I said, my R-sound neutral, plain. A pause and then, "Do you have sugar?" They looked at me like I was insane until we all burst into hysterical laughter.

"Jeanie, I'm home," I yelled, entering the apartment. She hadn't moved, sitting on the futon in my bedroom.

"They said one of the towers collapsed," she said, pointing to the TV. On the news, they were replaying footage of the South Tower collapsing, the news anchors animated and on, maintaining control. Its lone twin stood high above New York, bleeding smoke.

I brewed coffee, smoked cigarettes. I was making Jeanie nervous. I picked up the phone. It was dead. The North Tower of the World Trade Center collapsed at 10:28 a.m.

Time stopped. Hours passed unnoticed. We waited for our stray birds to flock home.

When Holly arrived, I opened my arms to her. There were faint, white ashy streaks on her smart, earth-tone business suit and her sensible brown suede pumps. She cried unabashedly as she walked up the stairs. She entered our home and sat down at the kitchen table. I put a glass of water in front of her and handed her some tissue. She took a pack of Marlboro Ultra Lights out of her bag and lit one.

"I'm tired," she said.

"How'd you get back to Queens, Holl?"

"I walked over the bridge. Took the bus."

"The buses are still running?"

"Yeah. They're not charging a fare. Just letting everyone on."

When we heard the door downstairs open, I jumped out of my chair and bolted. I threw open the front door. I threw myself at Jhess. She was sweaty, the vestiges of androgynous perfume clinging to her neck and short, wavy hair. Her messenger bag was slung diagonal across her full chest and she was wearing a sleeveless t-shirt which made her look tougher than usual. Her big black boots were scuffed.

"Whoa! What the fuck, kids?"

We all laughed involuntarily. The room came to life. We smoked cigarette after cigarette, pooled cigarettes, then smoked one another's cigarettes. Everyone was animated, exchanging stories, cursing freely, reporting, interrupting.

"I want to drive," Holly declared, her Woodside accent all determination. People would often ask her, "Are you from Brooklyn?" She'd respond, "Nah, I'm from Queens. But I get that a lot." She and Jhessika had met on the softball team at Franklin K. Lane High School and had been best friends since—Holly being Irish-surnamed and ethnically Lithuanian, and Jhessika ethnically Puerto Rican. "We've gotta go somewhere, let's go somewhere."

The sun had set and it was dusk, almost dark. It was very quiet, not only on our block but throughout the entire neighborhood. Beata wasn't home and it occurred to me that I had no idea where she worked or where Damion attended school. I looked up the sky. There were typically airplanes coming and going, flying low over Maspeth because of its proximity to LaGuardia Airport and JFK International, but at that moment, the sky was completely still.

We were silent in the car. The streets were deserted, empty, no one on the road. I hadn't bothered to ask where we were going. I didn't care.

Holly maneuvered the car onto Metropolitan Avenue and I momentarily turned to look back at Manhattan, the shroud of distance obscuring it. Right onto Fresh Pond Road, past the elevated M train tracks, left onto Myrtle Avenue at the trestle. The trees and their shadows formed a benign gauntlet as we glided through Forest Park. Exiting the park, she hit the brakes, twisting and turning onto Woodhaven, then slowing down to a crawl. We were on a tree-lined street of cozy houses with little fences and tiny yards.

"You okay?" Jhess asked Holly. She nodded wordlessly and rolled down her window, lighting a cigarette. She was slowly driving past her childhood home. The house had long since been sold, her parents long since divorced.

Woodhaven turned into Cross Bay Boulevard, a dull, broad road that became long and black, otherworldly. All the windows of the car were slightly open and the wind whipped our hair mercilessly. Soon the smell of the ocean became prominent. Houses and structures on either side of the enormous boulevard fell away and water flanked the road. The reflection of streetlights illuminated and sparkled on the black water stirring and shifting below. Holly pulled up at the boardwalk of Rockaway Beach. "I never find parking here," she mumbled.

We exited the car, slamming the doors in sync. There was no one around. I'd never seen Rockaway unpopulated before. We crossed the boardwalk and stepped onto the sand, leaving streetlights behind. The sound of the ocean greeted us. All turned to the rolling and roaring behemoth before us. Its repetitive muscular motion beckoned one to enter, to fall away into the nothingness of the water that reflected the nothingness of the sky, peppered by stars. Jhessika saw Orion. I smiled, seeing her face in the periphery.

New York had long ago been declared a no-fly zone. We looked out at the living abyss, its empty, wet mouth moaning, crashing, recoiling, as its pale spine folded backward onto its own mermaid's tail, a million coal-black horses disintegrated to cottony white froth upon contact with the shore. The sound unfurled in each direction—ancient, demanding, permeating all that belonged to it, save for the sky cut to pieces by the explosive sound of fighter jets overhead.

Three Poems

Nicole Cooley

Our Lady of the Millennium, Astoria, New York

The view from our apartment window is a puzzle

of clotheslines, yards and fences opening onto each other,
square after small square. Rigged on pulleys, ropes

of clothes hold the city together. In bed, in these last
weeks of the century, I keep the baby still safe in my body,

while the subway's a stage set, N train breaking
out of darkness into neon and hand-lettered signs—

Corfu Gifts, Green Card Lottery—into our bedroom.
We stand at the window, watching

the front garden's marriage of weeks and too-bright
flowers with lipstick names, Ultra Plum, Celebrity Pink,

Broken Heart. Up the street, the Nursery cuts cones
of wedding roses and shapes baby's breath into a cross.

In our yard, a stone virgin stands alone, blue-robed,
arms open, blessing the sidewalk, the subway tunnel's

rusted ribs, this other world outside the house where we
are waiting, our grip on each other holding tighter.

The avenue is a bed that rolls and pitches while
the stone woman waits, her body driven straight

into the dirt for luck or hope or *home,*
this world washed gray, lit by our bodies, not heaven but

a landscape we can't map—happiness.

Photograph #2, Queensboro Bridge

The sky salt-white. The rails scrawl
across the water, a barge piled high with tires.
First the shock that there's a world
beyond my body. First this landscape
outside the magnetic field I can't step into,
tube of light where my child lies,
small fists tied down, fairy tale oven.
I don't want to see it so I watch
the green-black water, remember
a butterfly clip pinching a vein
open, needle of wicker-colored fluid
spilling my body's secrets, promising
faith. The only promise is that the self
will be crowded out of the body.
That the bridge scripts the river.

For Joseph Crowley, 7th District, New York, Bronx and Queens

Not the city's center but its edges—Sunnyside Yards where
the train finally rises from the tunnel where ice clots
on grass scattered with trash.

The city would speak but it is currently preoccupied with
    its own defense.

Not the blue arterials on the midtown map.
Not the escalator in the train station threaded
with camouflage, guns slung over shoulders.

No—the trenches beyond the tracks—
shopping carts overturned on their spines, six-packs
of smashed Corona.

These streets that do not appear on any news conference.
These neighborhoods that are unpatrolled.

This part of the city does not have a forecast for its future.
The view from the subway window makes its argument:
don't have another child.

The Sunnyside Shuffle

Ron Hogan

This was supposed to be a charming essay about living on the outskirts of Lewis Mumford's ideal community, just two blocks down the street from the apartment where jazz pioneer Bix Beiderbecke spent his final days—a reflection on local spirits and their subtle influences over the neighborhood. I'd talk about how my aspirations for a quiet home with access to all of Manhattan's cultural amenities lined up with Mumford's theories of urban planning, and how Bix spoke to my creative side; then I'd throw something in at the end about how Starbucks had come to Queens Boulevard but we hadn't changed all that much, not really.

That was before the bedbugs showed up.

When I moved to New York City in the summer of 2000, I picked out an apartment just off Smith Street in Brooklyn's Boerum Hill, then a very hip, up-and-coming neighborhood. Eighteen months later, as the lease was about to expire, I invited my girlfriend to move in, but she had a one bedroom in Manhattan just three blocks from her office, so I wound up moving in with her. By early 2004, on top of Manhattan rents being what they are, we were beginning to feel cramped, so one night we took the 7 line out to Sunnyside to look at apartments with a broker.

The first place she showed us was a small two bedroom in a converted home, decent enough but nothing spectacular. Next we went to a building where the hallway outside the one-bedroom apartment had burnt-out light bulbs, but that was okay because it obscured the fire damage to the walls. We liked the third place we visited, though—the living room and bedroom were each just a little bit bigger than what we had in

Manhattan, the kitchen was a separate room rather than a counter off
to the side of the living room, and it even had something of a foyer. All
for about half the rent.

We went to IKEA and bought a bunch of furniture we hadn't had
room for in the old apartment: five new bookcases so we could finally
unpack all my books, a new chest of drawers all my own, a kitchen table,
and a desk for my workspace up against the living room wall. It wasn't
perfect; we heard, and then saw, mice running across the bedroom floor
late at night, and as far as we could tell, our upstairs neighbor reenacted
the siege of Leningrad in heavy combat boots across her bedroom floor
every night. But we got two cats, the mice disappeared, and, as far as
we could tell, somebody else moved into that apartment eventually; all
they ever did was play really bad '70s music too loud in the afternoons.
Apart from one night, when I went downstairs to ask *that* neighbor to
turn down his stereo and wound up dodging his fists down the length
of the hallway, we were doing all right.

Mostly. At some point the hot water became ridiculously inconsistent,
just about vanishing altogether in the kitchen sink and only turning up
in the bathroom sink after I'd run the shower for at least five minutes.
Then there were the multiple floodings of the bedroom closet from a burst
bathroom pipe four floors up. But those problems were ameliorated by
the fact that, once you got past the building's problems, Sunnyside was a
great place to live. Our apartment was a short walk away from the 7 line,
which put us in Grand Central Station in about twenty minutes (except
for that time the MTA went on strike, or all those weekends and off-peak
weekday afternoons when they shut the line down for repairs). We had
a well-stocked grocery store on one corner, an even better supermarket
just down the street, even a Stop & Shop on Northern Boulevard if we
wanted to take a ten-minute walk. Our options for dining out were just
as excellent: Pick a regional cuisine, and nine times out of ten, you'd find
a place that served it. We had a Turkish place six blocks away that was
so good, the restaurant critic for the *New York Times* went there when he
just wanted to hang out and relax. If you walked twenty minutes, you'd
find the best Thai food in New York City, for way less than it would cost
in Manhattan. Gentrification came, slowly—I mentioned the Starbucks
on Queens Boulevard, right?—but for the most part, Sunnyside retained
all of its neighborly charms.

Which is why, when my wife first asked me in the late spring of
2009 if I'd been feeling itchy at night, I didn't think about it all that
much.

It's a pretty straightforward deal: you live in New York City long enough, you're going to hear bedbug stories. If you've never dealt with them before—like, say you spent your twenties living on the West Coast, in cities where bedbugs had been virtually eliminated by the 1990s—other peoples' accounts feel somewhat abstract, even when they're sitting next to you at a bar, explaining how they left their slashed mattresses on the sidewalk. Once you start waking up with clusters of little red bumps on your forearms and your ankles, though, a near-existential frustration sets in, intensified by the number of fellow New Yorkers ready to tell you how much they understand your pain.

The Sunday after Laura finally found a live bug crawling across the bed sheets, we went to Sleepy's to order a new bed. The store manager politely, almost cheerfully, informed us that Sunnyside had one of the fastest-growing bedbug problems in the five boroughs. (Oh, and the usual free removal of the old mattress? No way; they didn't want to go near that thing.) That didn't make Laura feel any better about continuing to live in the neighborhood, and she suggested that we start looking for an apartment in the uppermost reaches of Manhattan, or even New Jersey.

I favored a more cautious approach, suggesting we go through the bug-killing process first and see what happened. The following Friday, we got up early and, with the help of a neighbor, I dragged our two mattresses down to the sidewalk before the exterminators arrived; we could tell from the massive dark stains where the bugs had made their base camp. The exterminators went over the bedroom and the living room; they found a couple of bugs on the couch, as well as along a gap in the wall just above the bedroom floor. Six hours after they left, Sleepy's dropped off the new bedroom set, which we promptly sheathed in mattress condoms.

Things were a little better after that day, but only a little. We'd sealed up all our clothes, and just about everything in the living room, into large clear plastic bags, and for the next six weeks, those bags sat in piles on the living room, bedroom, and kitchen floors. We had to walk around the damn things just to get anywhere—not to mention all the books I couldn't get at because they were sealed up in plastic. But that would've been bearable if I knew that we could unwrap everything at the end of the six weeks and the problem would be solved. Unfortunately, halfway through, I was stretched out on the couch reading one night when I happened to spot a bedbug hustling along the edge of a back cushion.

We figured out that we weren't the only people in the building who had a problem with bedbugs. In fact, our next-door neighbors had come out into the hallway during the exterminator's last visit, asking him to come in and do *their* place. The whole no-real-hot-water thing had left us with little confidence in the landlord's ability to get the problem solved, so we'd called in our own exterminators, but within a few weeks, the bugs had shown up in enough apartments that the building's management was sending their service to the units that had asked.

If you've ever dealt with bedbugs in an apartment building, you know: You either do the whole building, or you're just pushing the bugs behind the walls from one unit to another, and eventually they'll wind up back where they started. Once we found them in the bedroom again—though thankfully the mattress condoms had kept them from actually re-infesting our new bed—we made up our minds: Screw the lease; we were out of this building at the first opportunity.

Still, I wasn't ready to abandon Sunnyside, and once we started talking seriously about where to go next, Laura didn't want to leave, either. A new wine-and-tapas bar had just opened at the end of our block; we had a solid selection of take-out menus we could rely on, and we had just found an Asian grocery store three subway stops down the line that sold phenomenal fresh vegetables. We knew we would be hard pressed to find another neighborhood this amenable to our needs, and another apartment with this much space, anywhere this close to Manhattan.

I was open to the possibility of a new neighborhood, but I felt more comfortable in Sunnyside than I had at any point in my adult life. It wasn't just that I'd been in this neighborhood longer than anywhere else I'd lived since graduating college, although I'm sure that played a major part in the bonding process. I liked everything about Sunnyside except the particular building in which we lived—if we could just change that, I'd be all set.

Laura and I went back to the broker who'd found us that first apartment, five years earlier, and spent a Sunday afternoon in the early fall walking around Sunnyside again. Technically, the apartment we settled on, five blocks from our original location, puts us in the adjacent community of Woodside. Nomenclature aside, our new place has the exact same neighborhood feel—even better, because we're in a converted two-story home rather than a six-story apartment building—and we've even managed to gain a little extra room for about the same rent. (Instead of writing this essay jammed up against the living room wall, for example, I've got my desk set up in the second bedroom, which has been converted into a small office and holds four of the five bookcases we bought when we first came to Sunnyside.)

We've got a new grocery store at the end of this block; it's missing some of the things I most appreciated from our old store, but it's still very reasonably stocked, and the Thai place around the corner is even better than the one we used to order from. The cats freaked out at first, but they quickly adjusted to all the additional space. Maybe we're not so close to the Starbucks anymore, but we can live with that.

A little over a month after we'd settled in to the new apartment, we found a dead bedbug in the bathroom, and for a moment, all the old panic came rushing back. Once we'd calmed down, however, we called a local exterminator that offered a bedbug-sniffing dog; he came to the apartment early one Monday morning and his dog sniffed around all our walls and furniture and didn't turn up a blessed thing. We decided we must have brought the dead bug with us when we moved, and though we still haven't let our guard down completely, we've been able to circle back to enjoying life in Queens as much as we did when we first moved here.

Who knows? One of these days I might even get around to reading Lewis Mumford's *The City in History* (which I was supposed to read my junior year in college, but never finished) or tracking down some actual Bix Beiderbecke recordings. Or I might just continue to take this unexpected mash-up of suburban comfort and cosmopolitan diversity as it comes. Either way, I expect Laura and I will stay in Sunnyside for another five years, and then another five after that.

Eating East Elmhurst

Molly McCloy

I stripped off my belt and pried off my shoes. The classroom's radiators were blazing, the walls papered over with turkeys made from tracings of children's hands—strange birds, each with four dopey rounded feathers and a peppering of red glitter and gold stars. I stepped onto the scale and watched the red digital numbers blink and then settle at "142." Shit. I was up more than twenty pounds, a substantial chunk of weight that hung dead on my five foot one frame and spread ridiculously over my widening 38-year-old's hips. I hadn't weighed this much since junior high, back when I got called "fat girl" and regularly fantasized about gunning down my classmates.

My pot belly now rivaled that of Rick, the developmentally disabled guy my brother Bill had cared for at a group home back in Phoenix. Rick would always slouch back after a meal and let his beer belly pooch out, both hands resting on it, until Bill asked him, "Are you pregnant, Rick? What are you going to name the baby?" Rick would nod, pat his belly, and reply, "Chips."

"Peruvian *papas fritas*" or "*pan de bono*" or "*crema de coco*" would have been apt names for my own little belly-fat baby. Eating in Queens had given me love handles. Or, more accurately, life in New York had officially weighed me down.

I'd swaggered into New York four years prior, in 2003, fresh out of Phoenix and a short stint in Philly. All jacked up on my new antidepressant prescription, I felt indestructible. I'd pieced together my fantasy of life in New York based on my own late teens in Seattle and the romanticized

New York tales of those who had left the city in the '80s. I figured I'd
find my place in the gritty artist caste of Williamsburg or the Lower
East Side, and roam alleys and side streets with grungy filmmakers and
hairy conspiracy theorists. We'd roller skate across the kitchen floor of
some painter's defunct-pencil-factory-turned-freezing-squat. We'd talk and
smoke and drink all night and eat four-course, world-class meals at three
a.m., then sprawl out at sunrise on some soccer field on the East River
bank. I'd lie there in the itchy grass, feeling giddy and oddly cleansed
by that wiped-out, hungover state, as wide open and alive as I'd been at
age twenty-five.

There was one key difference between my delusions about New York
and those of the straight, early-twenties droves of Midwestern girls storming
Manhattan and demanding their *Sex in the City* cupcakes, Manolos and
Mr. Big meatpacking. Sure, we all wanted New York to notice us, love us,
and demand our presence, but as a dyke in my early thirties, I wanted to
be so cool that I didn't have to be beautiful . . . or even well-groomed.
The hosts of all the big parties would call and say, "Molly, don't you dare
hop in the shower or pick up that comb—we're sending the limo for you,
so you can get here right away." The headline in the *New Yorker*'s "Talk
of the Town" section would read, "Look beyond the beer gut and crow's
feet—McCloy is a genius." I had imagined myself reading my work in
the East Village or getting interviewed over West Village espresso. Instead,
here I was, sitting in a kiddie desk in East Elmhurst, learning ten ways
to say no to a donut.

These desks provided a particularly cruel form of humiliation for
the weight-loss group's members. Typical student set-ups with the hard
plastic seat and attached desktop arm, these seats were torture chambers,
fat-squeezing vises for the many group members who were over two
hundred pounds. A Jamaican woman in a gown-like green blouse and a
redhead wearing a smock and butterfly-print stretch pants both stuffed
themselves into the seats, the desktops bisecting their bellies. The balding
white guy in a button-down and the Latina with a mane of poufy hair
and name tag that read "Linda" were both pushing three hundred pounds
and knew better than to try the desks. They chose the only alternative
seating, plastic chairs at the back of the room where they couldn't help
but block the entry door, causing a bottleneck of people squeezing past
and bumping into each other. Debbie the weight-loss leader, an African
American woman in a shiny pantsuit, cleared her throat, uncapped
her magic marker and began to speak over the ruckus at the back of
the room, the grunting and the whispered apologies and the chair legs
scraping the linoleum.

"This isn't just a diet. It's for life," Debbie shouted.

The commotion at the back of the room grew louder for a moment. Linda was being crushed from the front and behind by people trying to squeeze between her and a classroom cabinet. The Jamaican woman tried to scoot her little torture chamber away from the whole mess.

"This is for life," Debbie shouted a bit louder.

"Oh, no," Linda groaned.

My two years in Park Slope, Brooklyn, were manageable since we were thirty minutes away from Manhattan, where I studied writing. I didn't really fit with the yuppie-mom stroller crowd, but there were plenty of lesbians around and I loved walking my dog in Prospect Park. Then we moved to Queens so my girlfriend Rebecca could attend CUNY Law with all the other public-interest dykes in the no-man's-land of Flushing, far away from any subway line. Out of school, MFA in hand, I graduated to the dubious status of law student's girlfriend, college-loan debtor, cash-strapped renter, adjunct-instructor-workhorse, and stymied resident of East Elmhurst, pushing forty.

At first, we picked Jackson Heights because living in Forest Hills would have been like living in a cemetery, and living in Rego Park would have been like living in a mall, and staying in Brooklyn would have meant two-hour commutes and no yard for the dog. We'd ruled out East Elmhurst as too far from the subway, but we called an ad that read, "two bedroom in Tudor, Jackson Heights," and it turned out to be a basement apartment/converted garage just a half-block into East Elmhurst from the borderline of Northern Boulevard. We took the East Elmhurst basement apartment because the landlord, Camillo, an Italian postal cop who wore a gun and blue uniform and cap that made him look like a 1950s bus driver, was the first of twenty Queens landlords to say yes to our dog and cat. He didn't blink when we said we were a couple and he didn't even check our credit.

Just before I signed the lease, a small cockroach crawled across the paperwork. Camillo said, "Really, that's the first we've seen, and we been here all day." He said it with that credible Queens accent, the doorbell whine punched with gummy consonants. Convinced, we signed on to East Elmhurst.

Our yard was about forty by fifty feet of brick patio, weed trees and morning glories, and was boxed in by other small yards, the whole area pulsing with some neighbor's salsa music. Three kids were constantly kicking a soccer ball against our shared chain-link fence. There were still some Italian families around, but our side of the block was solidly Latino while the other side was mostly Asian. The local park was filled every morning with middle-aged and elderly Asian women doing Tai Chi, and in the afternoons with Latino school kids playing handball. Soon Rebecca was gone all the time at law school and I was teaching at three different colleges in Queens. No wonder I started eating.

I could have easily done my damage at the KFC or the White Castle. Both fast-food establishments were three minutes away from my basement apartment. The wind would often blow KFC napkins and White Castle French fry sacks past my place on 88th Avenue, but I wasn't even tempted—eating at a fast-food chain restaurant would only encourage the nagging feeling that living in Queens was like no longer living in New York. Now that my subway ride to Manhattan was over an hour long, I already felt as though I were rotting away in some Iowa suburb. Instead of chomping on slimy sliders, I began eating at a wide array of ethnic restaurants, all within walking distance of my apartment, embarking on a two-year pig-out session artfully disguised as multicultural exchange.

In Queens, I ate rotisserie chicken and ceviche at eight Peruvian restaurants, sampled skirt steak with olive-oil-and-herb *chimichurri* sauce at three Argentinean steakhouses, and I tried three types of flan as well as churros stuffed with *dulce de leche* at the Paraguayan bakery. I ate sloppy tacos overstuffed with roast beef *birria* at eight Puebla and Vera Cruz–style taquerias. I neglected to try the Hungarian café but did some serious snacking at the Indian chat houses. There were Pakistani and Bangladeshi restaurants. Mexican, Filipino, Indian, and Asian grocery stores and a Cuban diner. I could choose between Indonesian, Burmese, Malaysian, and Woodside's famous Thai at Sripraphai, where the smell of fresh chili and basil would hit me as soon as I walked in the door. There were at least ten Columbian bakeries that served cheese-bun *pan de bono* with café con leche. Korean barbecue, Vietnamese, Afghan . . . the list went on. I could take a bus ride to Flushing, where there was an Asian business district not overrun with tourists like Manhattan's Chinatown, with incredible dim sum and fifty-cent dumplings and soups with mysterious floaters that I sometimes couldn't recognize as meat or vegetable. Another bus ride would take me to Polish pierogi or Uzbekistani food. An independent Ecuadorian snack bar that operated in Flushing Meadows Corona Park served slices of whole roasted pig with hominy to the hordes of local soccer players.

Certainly, this was the type of variety you could find spread all over Manhattan, but here in Queens, it was concentrated in specific neighborhoods and you had to ask for the check instead of being shooed away to make room for tourist groups. The Mexican restaurants had menus in Spanish only and were filled with Mexican customers. Ethnic restaurants were filled with people of that same ethnicity. Queens cooked for itself.

At first, the eating was an excellent escape. After a routine publishing rejection, I'd have coffee and *pan de bono* at Natives. I took a big orange booth right by the window, sipped a giant mug of coffee with hot milk, ate *huevos pericos*, and watched people out the big picture window, as waiters glided by in black and white outfits, sharp like tuxedos. And, oh, the *pan de bono*—the cheese was worked into the dough before the buns were baked, making it a buttery, cheesy delight. The *New York Times* lay spread out on the table between my girlfriend and me.

When my neighbors stole three months worth of my Wellbutrin out of the mail and then tossed the empty bottles into our yard, I headed straight to Pio Pio for fabulous rotisserie chicken, fresh-cut French fries, piles of fried fish, ceviche, and the oily goodness of Spanish rice and beans. I smothered it all with this creamy and spicy green sauce, made with some secret addictive spice.

Then there was the time I received an e-mail with the subject line of, "You won the college writing contest!" but the body of the letter was addressed to some other student in the class. To kill the disappointment, I hit Sripraphai with its curry noodle soup, fresh herbs and searing chili, and frighteningly authentic menu that made me feel worldly, even though I didn't order the offal or pig snout.

Constructing my identity of international connoisseur was a relief, but I couldn't escape for long. I was teaching six classes at three different colleges in Queens. Instead of chomping on *dosas* and slurping up curries, I taught classes jam-packed with students like Yenifer Cabrera, Suyeon Hong, Mohammed Ali, Ibezim Iwu, Baruch Krieger, Akissi Kouassi, Hanifa Sharzai, and Iqbal Singh. Instead of ordering mango salad with lime juice and a whole steamed fish slathered with basil, I dealt with Madian Ali and Shemona Dalrymple coming to class late, Nester Deleon leaving early, and Nadege Innocent and Darshan Patel not showing up at all. Go Woon Park refused to talk in class, while I often had to shout over the constant commentary of Shantaya Junier, Titiana Jackson, and Niftina Jones. I had the hardest time with a pack of five girls in my morning class. They'd foment chaos any chance they got, sauntering in late and walking right in front of me mid-lecture, taking us off topic just to insult a classmate with covert slang and interrupting other student's comments by raising their hands so high while whining like frustrated puppies, until it was their chance to speak. If I didn't play it right, these classes turned into *The Jerry Springer Show*. And I didn't even get to be Jerry.

They were loud-talking, tough girls and I wondered whether at least some of them were lesbians; I'm sure they wondered the same about me. The most butch of them would defend me as she slouched next to a girl

I assumed was her femme girlfriend. Wearing a baseball cap with its flat brim jutting out and some loose-fitting sports jersey to look just like the hip-hop guys, the butch girl would slump back and say, "Nah, McCloy's okay." Then, and only then, the group would allow me to lecture.

It all came to a head one day when, in the middle of writing lab, the loudest of the five girls, who went by the misnomer Serena, slid up close behind me. I could feel Serena's breath on my neck, the rustling of her clothes and jangling of bracelets, and I turned just in time to catch her gyrating, a celebratory bump and grind of the pelvis, both of her arms held triumphantly above her head, fingers snapping out the beat.

"What the hell are you doing?" I said. I'd had a hard time teaching in Queens, but this was the first time a student had attempted to dry hump me.

Serena stopped and stared at me, her mouth in an "o." The pack of five waited for me to make my move.

"I guess I'll take that as a compliment," I said carefully.

Serena flew right back into her dance and then pointed at me in rhythm, a Mick Jagger stage antic, as she warned me, "Yeah, take it like a compliment, B—"

A cell phone rang. With a loud jangle of bracelets and keys, the group gathered up bags and books and rushed down the hall, laughing and hooting about something else.

"Don't forget the homework," I called after them.

Faceless in New York, overwhelmed in Queens, fat in East Elmhurst, I finally began dragging myself to the weekly weight-loss meeting in my neighborhood. My girlfriend and I had to walk past a lot of tempting East Elmhurst food on Northern just to get there. First, there was the KFC and the Peruvian restaurant; then the Mixtos stand, where beef or chicken or both were stuffed into arepas; then Mama's Empanada's as well as Papa's Empanadas, with their fried corn or flour pockets, stuffed with any savory item you could think of, and the amazing sweet potato empanada dusted with powdered sugar. There was Hamburger Extasis, with its garish, food-porn photos: eight-by-tens of hot dogs loaded with onions, beans, and mayo and gooey cheeseburgers with potato chips tucked under the bun; the *cholado* stand, where fruit juice was mixed with condensed milk and ice; the *carniceria* and the Argentinian steakhouse, both with skirt steak on the grill.

Debbie, the weight-loss leader, got heckled at every meeting. The most common complaint was from women who said they had done everything right, had counted their points and exercised, and still the number on the scale refused to go down. "It's not working," they'd grumble. "I feel ripped off," they'd complain. Faced with yet another cutesy acronym on the flipchart, someone in the back would yell, "Oh, what's the use?"

In the face of this type of complaint, Debbie would throw up her hands and give a throaty shriek. "What do you want me to do about it, Esther?" she'd yell at Esther. Or Clarice. Or Harriett. And then she'd pause and shoot us all a bug-eyed, cartoonish face, her hands frozen on her hips. After a moment of the cartoon pose, she'd turn back into our leader and discuss plateaus and muscle weight.

At my third meeting, Debbie read the group an inspirational quote from a breast cancer survivor that had been included in some weight-loss group literature. It was something to the tune of, "Live every day, sing every song, dance every dance, like it's your last." It was the kind of trite saying that might be printed in pink letters on positive-thought-for-the-day calendars.

"She got cancer because she lost weight, or she lost weight because she got cancer?" a woman with a thick Russian accent asked Debbie.

"Huh?" Debbie said.

"It's her own fault that she got cancer," the Russian decided.

"Huh? Did I say something about cancer? This is about *dancing*. Let me read it again."

Debbie had forgotten the little footnote about the cancer, but apparently that footnote was the only part the Russian had understood. Everyone turned to look; the fun, now, was to figure out if there was just a language barrier or whether mental illness was also at play. The Spanish speakers looked over for a moment and then continued their usual huddled whispers, a private conversation. Debbie read the quote again: "Live every day, sing every song, dance every dance, like it's your last."

"I'll need another name tag," the Russian said. She lifted her chin and gave Debbie a proud and defiant look. "From now on, call me Moon Beam."

Debbie didn't miss a beat. "Alright, Moon Beam. Today's topic is: 'How to say no to a croissant.' "

"Not a crescent. A full moon," said the Russian.

It was around this time that I arranged for my critical thinking class to do some oral reports. I had tried everything with this class, splitting them into groups and refraining from whole-class lectures, which worked fine for my other sections; nothing seemed to work. So I decided to see how they liked getting up in front of the whole class to do some group oral reports on the Jena 6 case. I hoped that my students would realize how burdensome it was to teach such a boisterous class and they would calm down a bit.

I took my place in the back of the room, to watch how my hecklers would respond to being heckled themselves. The presentations were as chaotic as the audience response: pop soundtracks drowned out anything else going on in the PowerPoint, trite quotations about peace and love, misspellings on every frame, font that disappeared in background images of a matching color, long interruptions by the audience, dancing. It was half Dada and half variety show, and almost none of the presentation or questions were about the Jena 6.

"You like 50 Cent? Me too."

"Where did you buy that cute belt?"

"Come on, come on, admit it; everyone's racist!"

The class applauded. The presenters smiled and bowed. As class ended and several students waved goodbye to me, I realized I was the only one who thought the class period had been a disaster. The presenters hadn't felt disrespected at all and the audience had been satisfied. *Call me Moon Beam,* I thought. The sage advice of one of my students rang in my head: *Relax, Miss Molly.*

During one weight-loss meeting, Debbie called out for group members' success stories. A tall, pear-shaped woman named Roberta gave her total of two pounds for the week, and then her lifetime total of "over one hundred pounds." When asked to give one simple tip that had helped her get through the week, Roberta revealed that she would now go out and get one slice of pizza, whereas in years past, "I would get a pizza delivered and eat the whole thing myself."

There was something raw and vulnerable about this statement, coming from someone who didn't want to reveal her exact weight-loss total: loneliness leading to lack of self-control, and next, the humility required to take baby steps to rein in the self-destructive desire. Something about the image of this smart, no-nonsense woman, sitting on her own in her home and shoveling down a whole pizza, made me think of *me,* alone in my house and beating up on myself. If only there had been this type of honesty and vulnerability in my Manhattan writing classes, where memoir meant bitching about your family and critique meant tearing each other's work apart. I clapped for Roberta, and then I began to clap for the other women, too.

I offered my support with a sport fan's gusto, elbows raised, a boisterous two-handed clomping for the two-hundred-pound secretary who'd lost a half-pound. For the one-hundred-eighty-pound former P.E.

teacher who lost two pounds, I gave a "yay" and kept up my applause for so long, the group had to start up their clapping again. Rebecca stopped me from giving a standing ovation for the woman who gave her lifetime weight-loss total of ninety pounds, but she wasn't fast enough to silence my rock-stadium "woo-hoo!" I even teared up a little; I was inspired. Forget fame and fortune; New York was the city of hassles, where it took a Herculean effort just to cross the street against the crowd or deal with the laundromat or get your mail forwarded. Forget New York's artists, musicians, poets; the fat housewives of East Elmhurst were my new heroes.

Rebecca and I began eating well in East Elmhurst. Ceviche and avocado salad and a beer each at Pio Pio was pretty good on calories, as was the whole steamed fish and mango salad full of lime juice and herbs at Sripraphai. We began to learn how to make some of the dishes from Inti Raymi, like the cilantro chicken soup. We could even split the skirt steak at the Argentinian steakhouse if we went easy on the *chimichurri* and had the steamed broccoli instead of the French fries. We made the mango salad by buying crates of yellow Haitian mangos at the Indian grocery store. After four months of dieting, I could run more than a mile, and I could do eight pull-ups.

I steadily attended my weight-loss meetings each week, partly because the plan was working and I was getting leaner and stronger, but mostly because Debbie knew how to keep us entertained. One night she spontaneously stripped off her clothes to reveal her workout outfit, a 1980s leotard with belt. In another meeting, she passed out ten years' worth of her daily food journals. "You were eating a lot of bagels in June, 1999," someone taunted. "You were eating a lot of bagels in October, 2001, too," someone else chimed in.

After six months, I reached my goal weight by losing twenty-two pounds and then spent six weeks maintaining it. In early June, Debbie called my name and I stood at the front of the classroom with her, ready to receive my lifetime member award. Roberta gave me a thumbs-up and smiled. Lorraine, the Jamaican woman who always wore that same green outfit from the first night, gave me a nod. Esther and Clarice, the cranky senior citizens who often functioned like the two critics in the wings of *The Muppet Show*, were chatting about something else entirely.

Debbie was about to hand me my symbolic trinket when Linda muttered loudly, "She didn't have anything to lose in the first place."

Great. Now I was too skinny. But Linda had a point. I'd set and met this goal that was easy in comparison to the fifty-pound or even one-hundred-pound goals of other women in the group. The rest of the group began murmuring in agreement or disagreement, as Debbie took up the bug-eyed, hand-on-hip pose.

"Maybe if we all started coming to a meeting back when we only had twenty-five pounds to lose, we could all be standing here with Molly," she said. The group went silent. "Mmmm-hmmm. I *thought so*," Debbie said, hammering home her point.

I squeezed my way back into the crowded classroom and slipped into my kiddie seat. The conversation moved on to something else, but I closely watched my defender Debbie. How did she push back against her audience? How did she carve out space, even if she held it only for a moment? I watched Debbie work her slapstick postures. The rubbery expressions of mock umbrage. The exasperated shrieks. Here was one way to deal with the crowding of New York, the chaos of Queens. I took careful notes.

High Q

(excerpted from a collection of Queens-based haiku)

Roger Sedarat

Author Background

Like Don Quixote, though hardly with any literary significance, the Iranian-American poet *Gowje Farangi* ventured out into the world full of illusion toward the end of the twentieth century. After graduating from college in Austin, Texas, and failing to land the big recording contract with his punk band, Café Flesh, he cut his hair and sold most of his belongings, including his amp and microphone, and moved to Queens.

It matters little that he lacked the credentials at the time for the serious study of poetry. What's important here is that he saw himself on a kind of spiritual pilgrimage, not unlike Bashō. Modeling himself after this master—who took his pen name from the banana tree outside his hut—this aspiring haiku artist adopted his name from the tomato plants he grew outside his illegally rented basement apartment in Rego Park, Queens (*gowje farangi* means "tomato" in Persian).

He liked especially that the Persian name had "*farangi*," meaning "foreignness," in the title, as he saw himself as an outsider in this new land. So different did this part of the diverse East Coast appear compared to his experience in the more homogenous culture of Austin, Texas, that during the orientation for the MA program in English/Creative Writing at Queens College (now an MFA program in Creative Writing and Literary Translation), he remarked, "This must be international day."

Little is known of *Gowje Farangi* (or *GF*, as he often abridged the name in his writing), before his mock-pilgrimage to Queens. Some unremarkable scholars, who years later turned their attention to his life in hopes of writing original doctoral dissertations, speculate that his original name was Haji. Significantly, no other works except a few other random haiku published in journals bare the roots, so to speak, of this poet aligned with an ephemeral plant that grew in shards of glass in the backyard of an idiosyncratic landlady who, to this day, describes how he looked in his sleep when she crept downstairs in the middle of the night just to double check that he was not, in fact, her husband who abandoned her years before and returned to his family of origin in Israel.

About Style and Theme

For the most part the poet in English honors some of the basic conventions from the Japanese haiku of simple language, seasonal references, etc., though technically speaking many of these poems more strictly qualify as *senryū* and at times get especially postmodern and tricky. It is surprising that given his supposed Iranian background, few have little to do with Persian language or culture. Though readers can only assess the poet's experience based on the lines included here, they might consider how a kind of foreignness beyond the Texan underpins the writing about Queens. If this poet indeed came from a hybrid background of the two rather disparate countries of Iran and America, it paradoxically makes him belong rather strongly to this borough, perhaps the most diverse place in all of the United States.

In order to better put some of the following haiku directly related to *Gowje Farangi* in context, a few notes based on interviews with distant friends, the landlady, and former professors have been included here. Wherever possible, notation has been kept to a minimum, so that the haiku, however brief, might speak for themselves.

I. Neighborhood and Commute

In 1995, *GF* moved into a basement apartment in Rego Park to attend Queens College. His writing reflects considerable attention to key signifiers of his new life on the East Coast, invested in the images around him. His haiku around this time begins to exemplify a version of the commute

in which the majority of those living in Queens participate. Compared
to his previous time in Austin, Texas, relocating to Rego Park was like
moving to Mars, as evidenced by his special focus on the different people
he encountered and the lifestyle he pursued.

> On 63rd Drive . . .
> The Holocaust survivor
> sighs at bruised apples.

> Summer morning run . . .
> Two loops around the graveyard
> and parked sausage trucks.

> Tough guys from AA
> laugh about wrecking their lives . . .
> Shalimar Diner.

> A ride home from school.
> Argy, a Greek grad student
> refuses gas money.

> Headless ducks dripping
> grease in a foggy window . . .
> Rush hour on Main Street.

> Hear the world speaking
> on a single 7 train
> for a buck-fifty.

> Rainbow colored bird
> in need of new batteries
> above Chinatown.

II. Education

Though rumors strongly suggest he moved to Queens for the love of
a woman, he soon made his pursuit of a literary education his greatest
priority. Following the same curriculum as most any English department,
Queens College, as well as the surrounding area, further offered *GF* a

richly complex environment in which to study. Airplanes landing and taking off from two major airports became constant background noise. The following haiku show how he continued the study of literature on his commute and incorporated it into such daily chores as mopping his basement, performing a kind of "method reading" of Melville's masterpiece.

>   Why learn global lit
>   when planes circling overhead
>   show Hollywood films?
>
>   Maureen, Vanessa
>   Natalie, Angie, Crystal . . .
>   Student's brass name rings.
>
>   Gypsy cab driver
>   with degrees from home country
>   attends night classes.
>
>   Breaks from *Moby Dick* . . .
>   Swabbing the dirty tile floor
>   with Lemon Pine Sol.
>
>   Joking with Russians
>   about French literature
>   in a Chinese shop.
>
>   Beat up Rimbaud book
>   pressed against a stale bagel
>   in a coat pocket.
>
>   The Q88 . . .
>   Reading Kafka's *The Castle*
>   by Lefrak City.

III. Food

Queens offers cuisine as diverse as its inhabitants, even for diners as poor as *GF*, who eked his way through his graduate program with student loans. Though he tended to remain in his basement apartment reading books, he did get out to sample the local fare. The reader senses the hunger he experienced in his self-referential haiku, as he's able to get much needed rest after eating cheap pizza. Sources suggest that he used gift certificates sent by his father, who recalled his love of fried chicken as a child, to treat himself to an occasional lunch or dinner. As in any region, food offers an opportunity for an observation of the local culture.

> Dreams of tea-smoked duck
> served at *Spicy and Tasty*
> keep him up at night.

> One-dollar slices
> every Tuesday afternoon . . .
> nap until evening.

> At Queens Center Mall
> KFC certificates . . .
> GF's only meal.

> Mocking the natives:
> "Cawfee, no suga', no cweame."
> Dunkin' Donuts.

> You just had dinner;
> Now you want a large popcorn?!!
> Guido at movies.

IV. Appropriation

Though he obviously was a shameless appropriator of other writers, cultures, etc., *GF* seemed to take issue with those who would claim Queens on false pretenses. Whenever possible he also greatly appreciated the blue-collar sensibility of the borough, due perhaps to his rumored background of working at a Wendy's drive-thru while pursuing his undergraduate education in Texas.

> Sorry Vincent Chase,
> you're so *not* Queens Boulevard . . .
> Watching *Entourage*.

Times Square trumpeter
plays "It's a Wonderful World."
(Satchmo lived in Queens.)

That Ramones T-shirt
on the Manhattan toddler—
made in China.

Doug Heffernan:
the new Archie Bunker.
(*King of Queens*)

Refreshing to walk
in a not so cool New York . . .
Summertime in Queens.

V. Class Difference

Though affined with the working class, sources suggest that *GF* also moved to NYC in pursuit of an especially uptown girl. How she tolerated his freezing basement, much less spent time in his neighborhood alone as he studied or attended classes, surely baffled him to no end. On some level, however, it does speak for Queens as one of the more democratic boroughs, where those working toward a better life might socialize or even marry those much closer to the American dream.

He walks the rich girl
to LIRR station
then takes the R train.

Woman pops zits
in make-up counter mirror.
"*GF*, Queens is gross!"

His girlfriend sleeping
in the bottom of the ninth . . .
Afternoon Mets' game.

"*GF* . . . will our kid
be born with an extra ear?"
Breathing basement fumes.

One pint-sized heater
for 1,000-square-foot room
warming her bare feet.

VI. Tomatoes

GF's signature haiku directly confronts the tragedy of his tomato plants.
Unbeknownst to him, for some time his landlady would sneak in the
backyard before he awoke and steal his tomatoes, letting them ripen out
of sight on her refrigerator. Though lacking signifiers of Queens, the
experience speaks to the somewhat raw existence of his struggle in the
borough, along with some joy in spite of the difficulties. His landlady's wily
ways further exemplify the street smarts required to make it in Queens.

Bees on the blossoms,
yellow-black stripes on stingers . . .
Rego Park school bus.

Late summer morning . . .
Where have the tomatoes gone?
Landlady chopping.

How could a rabbit
survive boulevard traffic
to reach tomatoes?

"*GF*, call the cops!
Some thief's stolen your namesake
right off of the vine!"

New Jersey stickers
on tomatoes at Met Food . . .
One dollar a pound.

God Lived in Queens

Jayanti Tamm

Queens was the perfect foil, the humblest foundation. Queens served as the mud from which the lotus flower grew. It was a sanctuary, a safe haven. With its proximity to the power cluster of Manhattan, Queens offered easy access without rigorous scrutiny. Unknowingly, it aided and embedded, corrupted and abused. It was all a grand illusion, the creation of a mad man.

But you didn't know that. Not for a long, long time.

As a child, Queens was the Holy Land, the improbable, impossible setting of legend. Blessed and sanctified, Queens was hallowed ground, the destination for pilgrimage, the deified refuge. Forget Mecca, Jerusalem or Tibet—god lived in Queens. This was not speculation or wishful thinking; this was absolute. God hand-picked Queens as his consecrated ministry.

You had been told this. Raised in a cult where doubting and questioning resulted in expulsion and shunning, your Guru, Sri Chinmoy, informed you that he was an incarnation of god in human form. You grew up, rejoicing and reveling in your urban utopia.

Rather than establishing his ashram in one of Queens' pockets of preened gentility—Forest Hills with its cobblestone courtyards and turrets or the leafy Long Island sensibility of Douglaston—your god chose Jamaica as his dominion. Far removed from the sparkling blue waters and silky white beaches of its tropical namesake, Jamaica, Queens, bore no resemblance to the lush Caribbean island. The Jamaica you knew thirty years ago was not a vacation destination. Its disjointed houses stared blankly upon marooned shopping carts and the carcasses of burned, stripped cars. This was your monastery, your permanent spiritual retreat.

The drug-scarred streets, the empty crack vials and the continual wails and whines of car alarms reinforced your mission—to save your soul and transform humanity. Jamaica's exorbitant crime rate—the highest in Queens and consistently in New York City's top three danger zones—solidified your total and absolute reliance on the Guru to protect you.

To be sealed by his protection you needed to renounce worldly attachments, accept a life of strict celibacy, and obey the Guru without question. To ensure the Guru's protection, you severed relationships to family and friends and all distracting forces dwelling on the dangerous outside. Casting himself as the savior in this brutal realm, he created the rules, your invisible boundaries. You happily disengaged with the world, closing your eyes and indulging in the warm, addictive brew of dependency. The Guru assumed the role of god and father, and you clung to him for shelter. In him and him alone, you sought comfort and protection.

Drenched by his protective powers, you zealously renounced doctors and medicine. You required his permission before embarking on any action until the automatic urge to make decisions with clarity of purpose sputtered and stalled. Eventually, you were no longer capable of taking care of yourself.

It's a risky proposition to offer total protection to five hundred disciples living within a scourged precinct, but for you, it created a thick, urgent need for the aging, bald man. You clung to his improbable mandates. Because of the threat of carjackings, muggings, and burglaries, you armed yourself the best way you could, carrying photos of the Guru in your wallet and wearing a ring with his image as a powerful amulet. You would be guaranteed safe passage as long as you prayed to him each time you ventured outside your communal house. With enough receptivity and faith, you were immune from attack; nothing and no one could ail, harm, or kill you.

The Guru relished hearing stories of your near-misses, the accounts of his omnipotent protective shield, disarming and repelling the would-be attacker. Near the end of the meetings, you joined the line of disciples shaking with gratitude to recount tales of lives saved by the Guru. *You were fiddling for the keys in your doorway and suddenly a man or group of men surrounded you, demanding your wallet. Then the miracle happened: you started chanting the Guru's name and instantly, like magic, they fled.* Failed abductions were his favorite stories. The female's breathless chanting with folded hands which led to her escape, never failed to excite the smiling and nodding, clapping and cheering Guru.

Queens was his sacrifice. He told you he was the sole levy responsible for preventing total destruction. Knowing this injected you with the smug humility of the rescued; you reveled in the exclusivity of the Guru's small life-boat.

As a disciple, you clustered, forming a tight hamlet, a two-mile radius in Jamaica, where hundreds of women in cotton saris and men in starched white uniforms lived, worked and worshipped. Entitled by being the Guru's chosen ones, you greedily claimed the neighborhood, spilling your righteousness upon every inch of the blighted area. Homeless men with frayed rope belts and plastic-bag shoes pawing through dumpsters reaffirmed your urgency at the enormity of your charge. You set out to work, but your mission was not humanitarian, building shelters or healing broken lives. Instead, the solitary recipient of your breathless service was the almighty Guru.

When the Guru took up distance running, you graffitied the streets with orange spray paint, measuring miles. When the Guru desired 149th Street to be named in his honor, you removed the official street sign, replacing it with one that read "Sri Chinmoy Street." When the Guru wanted to play a concert before a large audience, you plastered bus stops, store fronts, and school yards with posters, heralding the joyous news with buckets of paste.

Every April and August, you decorated Queens, dressing up its streets in glitter and sparkles, lacquering them in the dazzle of your homemade parades. From Parsons Boulevard to Hillside Avenue and on to Union Turnpike, you stopped traffic to celebrate your Master. Golden effigies of your Guru towered atop ornate floats while you—their foot soldier— marched in their shadows. You imagined the stares along the boulevards as rapturous envy of your tissue paper–crafted spirituality. The life divine, proclaimed by your hand-stitched banners, too unachievable for their fallacious lives.

Unlike charlatan spiritual leaders who resided in manor homes with white-fenced sculptured acres, Jamaica instantly erased suspicions of the Guru's mounting fortune. For the politicians, dignitaries, and celebrities who arrived to pay homage at the humble temple on 164th Street, the modest environs heightened the myth of the holy man. In the background, you devotedly poured your life savings, paychecks, and inheritance into his coffers. Although his real estate holdings continued expanding around the world—apartments in Hawaii, Switzerland, Puerto Rico—he never considered upgrading his base and losing the effective cachet of being the unassuming Guru from Queens. It became tangible proof of his authenticity that you rushed to display.

You were always in motion, fearing that if you paused, even for a few minutes, you might stall. You raced for his approval knowing his whims were unpredictable, your next task uncertain. On a rainy Tuesday, he'd invent an all-night relay race in Flushing Meadows Park, and off you'd go, shivering in the deserted miles of former swamp land, awaiting your turn to sprint into the dark. A balmy Friday night required more of a challenge. He decided that 150th Street, a three-tiered hill emptying itself into Hillside Avenue, was your next obstacle course. You'd trudge your way to the top, fighting the dense slope, then repeat until the miles amassed a marathon, or until the Guru grew bored—you never knew which would happen first. You were not to neglect the body. The body was the temple of your soul and excising your impurity, your stained self, was an essential part of your spiritual practice.

Rather than resisting your unabashed takeover of the neighborhood, the neighbors—the "outsiders"—remained optimistically welcoming. Struggling to keep their own families safe, the other residents, a mixture of immigrants—Greek, West Indian, Pakistani, and Brazilians—did not view you as a threat. You did not use or sell drugs; you did not drink or smoke. No hippie beards and shaggy manes—all the men had neat, short hair, and all the women were modest and demure. Your rituals did not fluster the outsiders; Jamaica was, after all, just a few stops of the stops along the F train to Manhattan, and for that, they had conditioned themselves to accept anything. At the very least, you paid attention to the upkeep of your neat communal homes and businesses by painting them a unified, unrelenting shade of blue.

You coexisted with the "outsiders," yet you pitied their tragic, ordinary lives and sought to generously share your blessings. All day and late into the night, your singing and chanting emanated throughout the blocks that surrounded your temple—the tennis court. When the Guru became infatuated with tennis, you pooled enough money to purchase an abandoned lot, an overgrown gulley on 164th Street that you hand-built into a clay tennis court designed to perfect his backhand and your faith. Towering floodlights, illuminated center court and the neighboring streets, and a PA system broadcast every sacred lecture or scolding; through light and sound, the neighbors were immersed in your spectacle. From their kitchen windows, the neighbors gaped over the fence at the special dais and throne upon which the Guru perched. In sharp winter winds and dense summer heat, you bestowed unlimited chances to receive the Guru's divinity. This was your charitable giving.

Before your temple resided in a tennis court, your sanctuary was a rented second floor of a dilapidated building on the corner of Hillside Avenue. You defended it like a wrathful deity, guarding your shrine against any and all invaders with mouse poison, roach spray, and buckets for the rain that bled through the leaks in the ceiling. From the gated windows, you gazed upon a Petrol-City gas station. Basking in its glow stood a Popeye's Fried Chicken where the employees greeted customers behind a wall of thick, bulletproof glass.

The first floor of your temple was split between Chino's Car Repair and a furniture store stocked with beds with neon headboards, hot pink pelican lamps, and love seats shaped like giant oyster shells. Outside, rolled carpets leaned against the building like tropical tree trunks. After several years of peace and security, the Guru was shaken when the police raided the furniture store below and confiscated bags of cocaine inside the discount mattresses. It was then that you sought a different sanctorium.

One of your mainstays in the neighborhood was a facility you adopted as your own. Jamaica High School, a troubled and overcrowded public school, served as your own track-and-field complex. Because the Guru envisioned himself a star athlete, he made you run. Gaunt disciples trudged around the loop for multiple days in epic ultra-distance contests. The black cinder track always left its stain, its sooty mark. You wore those marks proudly—evidence of logging the mandatory mileage.

The high school students witnessed the spectacle. They knew that the Guru's chauffeur drove up to, and sometimes even around the track. They knew the Guru's sacred Porta-Potty was reserved for him and him alone. They were used to women running in saris, the blue fabric sweeping against the black track—running with folded hands, running while carrying the Guru's photo, running all night—eventually, their bodies lying sprawled upon the in-field in the aftermath of battle.

The students did not know that armed with bolt cutters, you created a new entry way inside the chain link fence the school installed to keep you out. They also did not know that you buried the Guru's favorite pet lamb in a rosewater-drenched shroud at the grassy south end of the field. To them, the Guru was eccentric and unpredictable. They gawked from afar, but they never came too close.

You were hand-picked to serve as the Guru's private bodyguard. Direct access to him was blocked; no one could approach or speak to the Guru without permission. Everywhere he moved, you respectfully cleared a path, careful not to allow your impure, imperfect self to contaminate his aura. Armed with an umbrella to shield him from the elements, you awaited the Guru's car and escorted him directly to his throne. During meetings, you alertly scanned for any breach of the barrier between the audience and the Guru. You felt grateful the Guru was safe.

You also provided security for the "divine enterprises," the stores owned and operated by disciples clustered on Parsons Boulevard. A health food store, stationery store, flower shop, gift shop, and luncheonette provided a contact point for outsiders to connect to the Guru. Shopping there was a divine privilege. Customers deemed unworthy were locked out. When vandals busted the gates, smashed the glass, and robbed the register, you patrolled every night until the sky was sprinkled by dawn's glow.

Late at night, after the services, it was always a comfort, an extra reassurance to pass you on duty. Women were commanded to travel in groups and pairs. Never, ever walk alone. A woman alone was too vulnerable, too susceptible to attack. But it was there, in those muted hours stashed between twilight and dawn, that the one from whom you sought protection harmed you.

Your deity, the vision of holiness, your celibate Master—too pure to shake a woman's hand—secretly summoned you to his modest, blue, two-story house to strip off your sari, unwrapping the yards of silk before him like a present. Publicly, he segregated the men and women, forbidding even the briefest conversations; looking directly into each other's eyes was prohibited. Secretly, he avowed his sex would purify, enlighten, and save you. You knelt naked before the avatar who raised you, awestruck at your special blessing to service your divine father in this holy way. He was your everything.

Eventually, after guilt and struggle, loss and grief, you stumbled away from your insular neighborhood, your circle of worn blocks; your charred faith remained behind. Your spiritual idealism plundered and looted for decades, far too late, you understood that the real center of danger was never the "outside" world beyond the enclosed blocks in Queens that you had been raised to fear; nothing there ever plotted and schemed so stealthily and masterfully to deceive you. It was the one who promised to protect you who shattered and stole, corrupted and exploited.

In the end, Queens was simply another victim—too trusting, too reckless in its acceptance and allegiance to those who sought shelter within it. Queens had been an unwitting accomplice. It, too, believed it was part of a movement to unify, to transform the world. Naïve and idealistic, Queens, like you, so painfully aware of its weaknesses, imperfections, dents, and tears, was an easy target, a malleable fool.

How to Disappear Completely

John Weir

You should see the embarrassing poems I've written about him. Andy: a straight guy half my age. My former student. Lives with his mom. What was I thinking? After school, when I've been teaching late and reading student work, I walk from the Queens College campus to Forest Hills, two miles through the center of Queens to the Manhattan-bound F train at Queens Boulevard. The MTA is a traveling frat house past midnight, just the dudes slumped in their seats or tuned into headphones, holding Discmen delicately in their laps. In the early morning I go home with other men and scribble poems in the backs of books.

It's all I've written for months, these odes to him. I scrawled one on the flyleaf of a book by Vladimir Mayakovsky. Did I figure I was nineteen? "I Feel My 'I' Is Much Too Small for Me," the poem is called, a quote from Mayakovsky's "Cloud in Trousers."

I wrote another on the last page of Roland Barthes's The Pleasure of the Text. Yes, I'm pretentious. Plus, I'm teaching a course in postmodernism. It wasn't my idea. The students asked for it. They heard a rumor I was intertextual, and maybe it's true: I scribble poetry on Barthes.

"Cruising" is the name of the poem. "I'm on a concrete slab in front of Burger King," it starts, and then I want to tell you the time: 2:26 p.m., March 20, the last day before the first of spring, the year 2001. "I'm in East Elmhurst, Queens, New York, Astoria Boulevard, right below the flight path of LaGuardia Airport.

It's Tuesday afternoon, and the sun is burning off the winter chill. Yo-dudes drive by in SUVs pumping rap, their windows unrolled. Tractor trailers shift gears, blow smoke. "It's Good for You," a truck advertises.

Across the street, which goes both ways, east-west, the Cozy Cabin
promises "Show Girls Daily," its windows masked with cardboard. Uphill
from the Cozy Cabin is the *Salon del Reino* or the Kingdom Hall of
Jehovah's Witnesses.

God is watching, which is too bad, because I've been at the Fair, a
pornographic movie theater. It's at 91st Street, lurching over half a block
along Astoria Boulevard. Once a movie palace, now it's a Giuliani-era
smut house. That is, they show kung fu movies in front to hoodwink
the Vice Squad, but in back past the bathrooms are three large viewing
rooms screening porn. There's a room for girl-boy sex, a room for boy-boy
sex, and a room for interracial sex and chicks with dicks. Girl-girl sex
happens in the girl-boy room and in the trannie room. Boy-boy sex is
carefully confined, taking place on just one screen, quarantined as if to
protect not just others, but itself.

It's the only sexual kick that's uncorrupted by alternatives. Every other
brand of porn is polymorphously perverse. Sure, you'll never see two men
kissing in a straight porn film. But at least the girls get it on. And there
are group gropes in hetero porn where straight men watch each other.
Gay guy porn, however, is almost fascistically pure. There's no mixing of
perversions: two guys, or five guys, or ten guys fuck. It's humorless and
male. No pleasure outside of the penis. No pain, either.

I'm gay because I hate not women, but men. I'm terrified of men,
which means, of course, that I can't resist them. I'm dying to know how
it feels to be a man. I don't want to touch them, I want to become them.
Him. Andy's back. If I could press my face to his back, I'm sure I'd be
ready for God—for punishment or mercy. I want to be inside him, to
know how it feels to swing from that center. Held in by his muscles,
pinned and secure. His back, the small of his back. "My ass," he said
once, ruefully, meaning, "All my weight's in my ass." It was affectionate
and sorry. I want him to talk about me like that. Is that gay? I don't want
to be gay. Gay guys are different from men, and I want to be the same
as men, which is what "homosexual" means: "resemblance" not "desire."
I yearn for what I'm not.

I'm not Andy. I'm an untenured college professor in a dirty movie
theater that runs kung fu films to placate the police. They're shown in
the front of the house before a vast empty orchestra and a grand balcony
that is permanently closed. Men linger smoking in the orchestra's foyer,
lounging on puffy couches and chairs. You can sit and chat, or play video
games, or stand against the chin-high oak divider behind the last row of
auditorium seats, your head in your hands or your arms at your sides,
waiting for the fifty-year-old Irish firefighter in work boots and a Mets

cap to sidle up to you and let a polite and silent interval pass before he puts his hand on your ass.

The neighborhood is half black and half Latino, so the Fair is crowded with black men with shaved heads or smooth conks or dreadlocks, wearing sweat suits and business suits; and there are men from Argentina, Mexico, Brazil, Peru, Colombia, Ecuador, El Salvador, and the Dominican Republic. Married dudes from Merrick, Long Island, stop by on their way home from work. They're Irish, German, Italian, Greek, and Jewish, carrying attaché cases and wearing gold chains and gold rings.

The age range is forty to sixty. If young guys show up, they're often Vietnamese or Taiwanese or Malaysian. No one looks like me: doughy WASPy white guy dressed like a preppie in khakis and a Brooks Brothers shirt. In this place, I'm the "other," which means I'm from Manhattan; I don't have foreskin; I don't speak Spanish, or Russian, or Korean; I don't have children or a wife; I live alone; I'm unbaptized; I don't pray to God. Plus, unlike them, I'm, you know, "gay." Most of the men at the Fair would say they are straight. That's the story of my life since high school. Even in a homo jerk-off parlor, I'm the only fag around.

In any case, everybody plays it straight. Here's the game: You hang in the boy-girl porno room for an hour, lounging in the low-slung leatherette reclining seats or standing against the wall, smoking butts and talking with your buddies. Then you wander, just wander, first to the john, then across the hall and quickly as possible through the boy-boy room. You might linger in the trannie room for a minute, as if you were an anthropologist reading fragments of Icelandic runes. Finally, you turn casually and head to the video "buddy" booths in back, which line two long hallways. Each booth is the size of a janitor's closet in a New York City public school.

There are about ten booths along each hall. Today I shared one with my "buddy" Rico. I think that's what he said his name was, though it might have been "Ricky," or "Rocky," or "Rocco." We didn't have a language in common. I asked his birthday and he pointed at his watch. "Where do you live?" I said, and again he laid his index finger obscurely but definitely on the face of his watch. If I had been able to speak Spanish, he probably wouldn't have wanted to talk, conversation being, duh, not the point of human contact in a stroke parlor. Still, I like to get whatever information I can: name, age, native language, childhood home, astrological sign. Rico seemed to be close to my age, though he might have been fifty. He was wearing a gold band on his left ring finger. I figured he was a Pisces, because he liked to kiss.

If he wasn't my first choice, he also wasn't my last. The whole thing was an accident, really: my being in East Elmhurst at such an hour on such a day. When I left Manhattan this afternoon, I was headed for school. I was due to teach my evening class in postmodernism, where we were going to discuss Barthes's notions of "pleasure" and "bliss." I ended up at a porno movie theater because I got on the wrong train and fell in love with a couple.

They were Russian, and it was the Number 7. I meant to be on the R. I was buying lunch at Dean and DeLuca on Broadway near Houston Street, and there was an N/R station next door. My face buried in Barthes, I mistakenly got on the N. After crossing under the East River, the train rose above ground, which the R doesn't do. As soon as I saw daylight, I knew I was way off track. The N would take me to jail, not college: it ends a bus ride away from Riker's Island. So I switched for the local to Flushing, where I could get a bus to campus.

Except that I was hijacked by a guy on the Number 7 holding his girlfriend's hand. They were speaking Russian, which is odd, because Russian immigrants in Queens mostly live along the G or E or F or R, in Forest Hills or Lefrak City. So these two people were out of place. He had a widow's peak, and she was wearing wraparound sunglasses like Yoko Ono. She was small and fine and he was lanky and wired and stroking her hand. I watched him stroking and stroking her thumb with his hand. He held her fingers laced through his, and he rubbed her thumb with the side of his index finger.

What's the connection that happens between strangers on a train? I'm watching them, they're not aware of me. But they're causing the fuzz at the back of my head and the tight feeling in my stomach. It's like Ernest Hemingway watching a fish. Occupational hazard: As an English teacher, I quite Hemingway, or rather, Nick Adams in "The Big Two-Hearted River," arriving by train at a burned-out town, walking past acres of scorched timber, everything charred and ash—even the grasshoppers' bellies are black—to a bridge across a river. Seeing the water, he thinks, Well, at least the river is there. And in the river are fish, and they are arching out of the water and turning and moving their fins and slicing back into the current; and watching them, in his watching and in their being watched, Nick feels "all the old feeling."

He feels something watching a fish. Of course, the fish doesn't know, or care, about Nick's feelings. The fish is unconscious, oblivious to Nick. And just as Nick and maybe Hemingway take pleasure in looking without being noticed or known, so do I. Watching the couple on the train, my head is cottony and my belly is tight. I'm wondering how it's possible to, whatever, flush red, feel something, have a whole relationship with someone who isn't aware you exist. I'm hooked on people who don't see me. We're tied together, though I'm the only one who senses the taut line from my gut to her finger, his hand. The way he touches and squeezes and caresses her thumb is scary and exciting. It's too much, he won't leave her alone, he leans over her and grabs her free hand and doesn't let go. If I were her, I'd ask him to stop. But I don't want him to stop.

When they get off the train at Elmhurst Avenue and 90th Street, six stations ahead of mine, I'm pulled out after them by the strength of the connection they don't see or suspect. My following them feels involuntary, which is not to say I don't know it's invasive: I'm a grown man on my way to teach a roomful of graduate students about "pleasure" and "bliss," and I have turned, halfway there, into a stalker, a stealthy Hemingway quoter, a creep.

Out on the train platform, she goes on ahead, and for a minute I think they've separated, because he's suddenly alone. His hair is sandy brown and thinning in front and I don't think he buys his own clothes. The sheer shirt and the pants—white painter's pants tight at the waist— seem like her choice. He's got a brown mole on his right cheek, thick blunt fingers, wide shoulders, and a funny walk. He nearly skips after her when he finds her down on the street. There she is, ahead of him, and he races to reach her, putting his arms around her shoulders and neck from the back.

I know I'm being perverse. I want to call the police on myself. So I lose them, walking to 92nd Street and turning north, heading up through Jackson Heights to East Elmhurst, "accidentally" reaching the Fair.

You never "decide" to go into a porno house. Anyway, I don't. It's not like planning a trip to the mall. Suddenly, I'm here. "Oh, look, gay porn, who knew?" Of course, I walked here directly, if leisurely, all the while telling myself that it's a pleasant day to stroll through the neighborhoods of Queens. Forget that I've got class to teach in two hours. Until the last half-block, when I make a deliberate turn into the entryway of the movie theater, I'm convinced I have other plans. I'll stop at a pay phone, call Andy, pray his mom doesn't answer. "Yo, dude. I'm in East Elmhurst, which, to get here from Elmhurst, you have to walk *north*. Figure that." Then I'll snag a cab on Astoria Boulevard and reach school way before class.

Of course, there are no yellow cabs cruising East Elmhurst. And the route to Queens College, by way of surface roads, is blocked at almost every turn by huge highways. A cab would have to spin me a long way out of the way in order to come back a short distance correctly. You see my dilemma. Why not go jerk off? I pass through the theater's gaping entryway, under the giant marquee—"FIRST RUN IN QUEENS," it says, coyly, as if you could walk inside and catch the new hit with Ed Norton—pay my dough to the Indian man behind the ticket booth, spin through the turnstile, and enter the Fair.

Like all the guys, I start in the boy-girl room. But I can't watch porn for long. It wouldn't matter if Omar Epps were doing Benicio del Toro, or Drew Barrymore were smooching Halle Berry. Porno makes everything look like a training film for garage mechanics: in, out, shaft, piston. Is that all there is?

After a minute, I cross the hall, through the boy-boy room, past chicks with dicks, to the buddy booths. Lining the halls are maybe twenty guys, potential "buddies," mostly in their fifties, their faces creased as sharecroppers' in a photo essay by Walker Evans. Men with big hands and chipped nails, men with their hair combed carefully in place, men in blue jeans and parkas, plain men. I think of immigrants to New York in the early 1900s, when guys on their own in lower Manhattan got tired of putting off sex until the day they had money enough to send home for their girlfriends and wives. So they went to a huge beer house on the Bowery, where boys gowned like Gibson girls served drinks and then had sex for pay in rooms upstairs.

That makes public sex between men sound quaint and historic. But I'd be lying if I didn't admit that the Fair is depressing. With men, there's always a game, and the winner of every porno palace is the guy who gets to reject the most people. The victor today is an Italian guy who looks like a stand-in for Robert De Niro in *The Godfather II*. He's strutting, angular, groomed, compact, well-dressed, quick-moving, all business. If you glance at him, he frowns. Lighting cigarettes, checking his watch, he has convinced himself that he's at a board meeting closing a deal, or scouting leftie pitchers. Anything but prowling the oiled halls of a crumbling smut house for a guy who'll put a finger up his butt.

Here is how I know I'm not a man: Men are people who can stand completely grim and immobile for hours dreaming of sex. In strip parlors, they lounge at the lip of the stage not moving, while someone gorgeous squats naked above them, legs spread. Slumped in chairs in porno theaters, they sit inert as rutabaga bulbs watching naked people flash exquisite body parts across the screen. In the hallways of the Fair, guys stand still as if mounted on corkboard, maybe not even alive. Pornographic sex is obviously a sedative. It doesn't excite, it deflates. The problem with American youth is that they don't watch *enough* pornography. Mothers, if you want your children docile and depressed, send them to the smut house.

In other words, I'm walking around and no one is checking me out. Half an hour's gone. I'm running out of time. I paid $8.50 at the door. I want my money's worth of joy. Which is when Rico turns up.

I'm circling the halls for the seventeenth time, and he's in the corner, next to the fire door, and he looks at me. No smile, nothing that nice. Just a glance, our eyes meet, and that's my signal. Is he attractive? Sure, everyone's attractive. Especially when you're running out of time. I'm a fatalist with sex: If you happen to want me, I'm yours. Which sometimes gets me in trouble. Not here, of course, if "trouble" means falling in love. You don't fall in love in video booths, except for ten minutes, and I've got twenty. Rico steps into a booth and I follow.

So here I am, an English teacher still unable to define "bliss" but standing with Rico in a booth as big as a bathroom stall. There's a tiny TV screen near the door showing four channels of porn: guy-in-leather, guy-in-gym-shorts, girl-with-tongue-stud. The other channel is static. Sometimes men who go with you into a booth will watch the screen, not you, while you both jerk off. Rico puts his arms around me, hugs me, kisses my neck. I'm leaning against the wall. A knee-high bench is built into the wall, and I take off my coat and put it on the bench with my knapsack.

Inside my knapsack is a $7.00 tuna fish sandwich that I bought at Dean and DeLuca, thinking, "I'll save this for later." I didn't want to eat on the train, because I was lost in *The Pleasure of the Text*. Barthes kept talking about "hermeneutics," which is Greek for "interpretation," though it also kind of means money: it's from a root word for "assigning values to things you exchange." Rico has got his hand in my pants. He is rubbing my penis through my boxer shorts, which I bought at the K-Mart on Astor Place after Andy told me that he got all his underwear at "the pharmacy."

"What pharmacy?" I said.

"Any pharmacy," he told me.

Then Andy lifted his shirt and showed me his shorts, which, like all men in America under the age of twenty-eight, he wears above the waist of his jeans. There was the sudden aching gap of skin between his shirt and shorts. "Is not the most erotic portion of the body *where the garment gapes?*" Barthes asks, in *The Pleasure of the Text*, his words jutting into italics. Whenever you see "skin flashing between two articles of clothing," he says, "it is this flash itself which seduces." And quickly disappears, which is the true joy: knowing joy will end. In other words, bliss is loss. Desire is whatever you're losing.

"You'll lose money buying them anywhere else," Andy said, and he was right. K-Mart was selling three pairs of boxer shorts for $9.95, way cheaper than the Gap. I bought nine pairs. The pair that Rico is rubbing his flat palm against is white with red pencil stripes.

Then he undoes my zipper.

Suddenly there's a dead guy in the room with me. Not Rico, but my
best friend Dave, who died of AIDS in 1994. I'm Norman Mailer: mention
sex, I'm instantly thinking of death. Is that "sex-negative?" Whatever, I'm
a gay man who has lived in New York for twenty-one years—for these
past twenty-one years—and I have watched a lot of people die. Everything
reminds me of death. Why should sex be an exception? Dave died just a
few months before all the new life-saving drugs became available. He was
a mean bastard while he was dying, but up until the last few months of
his life, he was delightfully silly. Mention sex to David, and he came up
not with death but with a party game: "In the movie of your life, who
would play your penis?"

"Who is your penis?" Dave asks from the grave, which, considering
that I've got Rico's hand in my pants, is kind of wrecking the moment.
Placating Dave, I say, "Angela Bassett."

"That's cheating," Dave says.

"All right," I say. "Eric Stoltz."

"Eric *Stoltz?*"

"You know, sturdy, pink, supportive. Not the lead but often an
intriguing cameo. Better for television, really: small-screen, German-Irish,
completely functional, thank you very much, and secretly capable of wacky
outbursts. *Stoltz* means 'pride' in German," I add, modestly.

That silences David. He's gone. The dead want to name my dick, but
Rico, the living, is holding it, pulling it out of my pants. Now I'm a fully
dressed man in a booth talking silently with a ghost while a stranger in
jeans and a T-shirt gets my penis out in the open, poking naked through
my shorts and zipper.

And he tentatively touches it. Which completely banishes David,
thank God. I'm alive, and I won't lie: There's the wonderful encompassing
shock of a guy putting his hand all the way around your penis.

"What's your name?" I ask him, because if you touch my penis, I'm
in love with you, and I want to hear him speak, this object of my love.
I ask again, "What's your name?" He's just my height; his hair is fine
and brown. He leans back and pulls off his shirt, and there's a cross on
a chain hanging on his chest, and I'm thinking, "Jesus hung out with
tax collectors, who is He to judge?"

There isn't much hair on his chest. He's thick-chested. His belly
is big but solid. He undoes my pants and pulls my trousers and shorts
to my knees, and then he raises my T-shirt and shirt and sweater—I'm
wearing a powder blue sweater vest, which, my students say, makes me
look Republican—and kisses my nipple, the left one, over my heart.

Well, he's holding me. My trousers and shorts are at my ankles. "What," I ask him, closing my eyes, putting my arms around his back, wondering if I should take off my watch, which is big and blocky with the face on the inside, against my inner wrist. I'm scraping my watch across his back as I stroke his shoulders. But if I take it off, I'll forget it. So I harrow his back. His head is under my T-shirt and shirt and sweater vest. "What," I repeat, "is your name?"

Our video screen is tuned to boy-in-leather, who's saying, "Faggot, suck my dick."

I never understand the preferred conceit of gay male porn, which is that somebody has to not want it. There's one guy who's straight and won't do it, and a faggot who constantly does. Though I guess that's me and everyone I've ever loved. On the other hand, Rico kisses me. He comes out from under my shirts and kisses me on the lips. He kisses me quick, once, twice, wraps himself entirely around me, holds me as tight as he can, kisses me again. We're kissing for real, now, and I'm thinking, Well, I hope he doesn't have herpes. Then I remember that there are other things I don't yet know about him: his name, and whether he has a functioning penis.

I undo his fly, unsnap his trousers, unbuckle his belt, and push down his pants. He's wearing pink bikini underwear, which means for certain that he doesn't speak English. He pulls his underwear down, and I say again, holding his penis—I take it in my hand not greedily or expectantly, or as if it were ever my right, but with an air of what Tennessee Williams would call "tender protection," I guess I *am* a fag, I can't a strange man's penis without quoting Tennessee Williams—I ask him again, "What's your name?" And that's when he tells me, with his dick in my hand. "Rico," he says, or "Ricky," or "Rocco," or "Rocky," or "Enrique," or maybe he misunderstood, maybe he was answering another question that I didn't think I'd asked.

So now we're two guys naked to the ankles. Or, rather, he's naked, I'm not. So I get shirtless, too. I think sides are supposed to be even. I drop my shirts and sweater to the bench with my knapsack and coat, and we're both nude with our pants and shorts around our feet. He's sucking my nipples again.

"That's right, faggot," says the guy on the video, which is, like, flashback to high school. I hit the channel button and change to static.

Rico and I kiss for a long time. Out skin pressed together, shoulder to thigh, we kiss. He won't talk but he likes to kiss. My watch has a button that lets you light its face to see the time, and I press it: still an hour before school. I lean back. He's jerking me off. I hold his penis. He has lumpy testicles held up close to his flesh and his penis is shaped like him, blunt and big-headed, but, unlike him, oddly aloof. He's sucking my nipples like I have taken my only son in my arms and nursed him, my hand on the back of his head, saying, "Rico," over and over, "Rico," softly, and he doesn't make a sound, he's sucking my nipples. His penis is Willem Dafoe. It's part of the action but it doesn't belong in this film. It should be in a French film, not this sloppy human American thing in which a grown man suckles another full-grown man with pink bikini underwear tangling in his shoelaces. And suddenly Rico yells, or really, cries, and he comes on my thighs, and all over my discount K-Mart boxer shorts that Andy got me to buy.

He comes and I don't. I smile apologetically. It's an unwritten smut house rule that you both come at once, so your buddy doesn't have to get you off when he's already splattered. But Rico smiles wistfully, and then, kindly and patiently, he holds me with his arm around my shoulders and his head pressed to my neck while he jerks me off. He's watching, we're both watching me. Because in the second before I come—more smut house etiquette—I have to turn sharply away so that I blast, not on us, or on the bench where my bag is packed with lunch and Roland Barthes, but against the wall and on the floor, so no one gets slimed or soaked.

I'm done, we don't speak. He dresses quickly, but he waits while I clean up, which takes awhile, because my shorts are shot. They're wet with him. I have to remove my shoes, my trousers and shorts, wad Andy's boxers, wipe myself with them, and drop them on the bench, leaving them behind.

He watches and waits. When I'm dressed, he grins, hugs me, turns to go, reaches out, puts his hand on my face, his palm and fingers on my cheek—"Every narrative," Barthes says, "is a staging of the absent father"—and he touches my face. "Later, man," I tell him. He goes out the door, I close it, wait a second, lean against the wall, close my eyes, remember, remember his hand.

Because joy, for me, isn't just sex. Sure, I liked his touching my dick. But it would have been okay if he wanted something else, if he asked to be dandled or paddled or tweaked. There was a guy once who called me his queer buddy and told me to tie his work boots to his testicles. "Whatever, man," I said. I don't mind what anyone wants. The payoff, for me, the value-exchange, is in the moment afterward, when we're dressed again as men, and he can't speak English, and I don't speak anything else, and he hugs me, and it's like, "Yo, man, I'm so alone."

There's my joy, how men are lonely.

I'm in love with male loneliness.

Women are supposed to be lonely. I watched those movies when I was growing up in the '60s and '70s, every afternoon on Channel 7, 1940s Warner Brothers movies full of powerful women feeling painfully incomplete without a man—which, they would obviously never need a man in the actual world. Where could Bette Davis or Joan Crawford want from a man? I will never be as self-sufficient as those women. But the fiction was they were lonely, and their loneliness was dramatic, often histrionic, even hysterical, and they said they were nothing without men.

At the time, I believed them. I even grew up thinking I would be like them, a lonely woman missing men. Freud says we're all born little boys and only girls have to become something else, but that's not right; I'm sure I was a girl. And the difference between men and me is that I became a lonely woman and they grew into lonely men.

Now I want to be what men are, helplessly lonely. It's men who need other men. Can I have that moment with you? Can I have that masculine distance, disappearance, vanishing, absence, remove, aloofness, withdrawal, that silent moment after sex with someone whose name I don't know who sucked my nipples, held my penis, cried like a child, and spilled himself across my thighs? He was helpless in that instant. The best thing about sex is helplessness, the stuff you can't do. He couldn't not come. I mean, for a minute, he had to be in the room, with me. And afterward, he put his hand on my face and said, "Bye." In whatever language. And I said, "Goodbye."

Outside, on Astoria Boulevard, there's no cab, of course. I've got time. I sit in front of Burger King and eat my sandwich from Dean and DeLuca.

When I'm done, I walk along Astoria Boulevard to the Van Wyck Expressway, taking the beautiful curve of the entrance ramp into traffic. I'm a grown man fully dressed walking along an expressway. It's spring, cars honk, not happily; people think I'm an idiot. Getting off the highway, I climb over concrete dividers, cut through traffic on entrance and exit ramps, reach grass, come to the big empty parking lot of Shea Stadium, which is blue. Then I'm on Roosevelt Avenue, on a bridge that goes over the Van Wyck Expressway and under the Flushing Number 7 train. This is where Nick Carraway and Tom Buchanan got off the train to visit Tom's lover Myrtle in Fitzgerald's valley of ashes. It's now a junkyard for wrecked cars, and it smells of sewage and vegetable rot.

Spin around above the waste and you can get a whiff of industrial waste, and a panoramic view of, you know, the postmodern condition. Texts competing for attention, equally insistent. Identity built from contradictory fragments that lead away from your "self" into nothing. I become what I see: the bruise-red cars of the Flushing local sinking underground across rusted switches and tracks. Planet Earth the graying Unisphere. All the parkways and expressways, the bloodlines Robert Moses laid through the bog, curl over and around each other like live bait in a soup can. And a sign across the Flushing River says "Self Storage."

And if I could have talked to Rico I would have said, guy-like, "Man, I love Queens." I love wreckage and disaster, industrial waste. I love looking at this intersection of highways and trains and planes taking off overhead and cars crashed and the river stagnant below and thinking this is all we can do, this is the best we can ever do, we get off the boat from faraway. places, slaughter the people living along the banks of the rivers and streams, and build across the new land a redeemer nation of what? Sewage, slop, waste, rot, rusted steel, the gaping awful failure of a century. Face to face with man's capacity for wonder and we make ourselves, in Flushing, a mess.

Not Manhattan's mess. Manhattan is the pores of the face scrubbed clean with astringent. The rest of the body is here, God's blood and guts and soul and wounds and all. I love the failing body, knowing we'll die. I love the clogged river and the deafening airplanes and the Mets, the fucking Mets. Because the other thing I want to be is nothing, I want to be lonely and nothing. Queens is a good place for that. There are lonely men everywhere here waiting to leave you so they can get close at the last minute. That's bliss. That's when I feel joy, when I want to be "present." David, while he was dying, was forever asking me to be "present." Well, here I am: leaving you, drifting past, hand on your face, reeking of come, headed for nothing, happy with that. It won't take a moment. Andy. Just give me your hand.

Snow Forts

Robert Lasner

Brian blows against the glass until it fogs up. Then he puts his lips against the glass like he is giving someone a kiss. Unlike someone's lips, the glass is cold. He pushes his entire face against the window, to get as close to being outside while still being inside. Beyond the cold glass is "snow, glorious snow," as his daddy sings in the car when it is snowing and he is happy. Snow, glorious snow, which Brian can roll in; snow, glorious snow, which he can play in with Kevin; snow, glorious snow, which he can eat when no one is looking.

When he is bored of pressing his face against the window, Brian jumps into bed and turns on the radio to listen to the weather report. "You give us twenty-two minutes, we'll give you the world," the man on the radio announces. When Brian is a grown-up like daddy, he is going to be a weatherman because a weatherman knows the weather before everyone else does, and when he is a weatherman, he too will know the weather before everyone else does. He will know when it is going to be sunny before everyone else does; he will know when it is going to be cloudy before everyone else does; he will know when it is going to rain before everyone else does; and best of all, he will know when it is going to snow before everyone else does. He will be able to walk into daddy and mommy's room and say in a loud voice like daddy's loud voice, "I predict there will be six inches of snow tomorrow." Just like the real weathermen on TV. And daddy will smile at his prediction, and tell him that he is a "good weatherman, a goddamn good weatherman." Daddy's favorite word is "goddamn." He says it a lot when he is driving in the car.

The man on the radio talks a lot about the snow. He says it is the top story. "This has been one of the worst snowstorms in New York City history," he says, "with a foot and a half of snow blanketing most of the metropolitan area, accompanied by dangerous winds which have gusted to over eighty miles per hour at times. Officially, seventeen point seven inches of snow have fallen in Central Park, though the Sanitation Department has reported that one of its stations in Southern Queens measured an accumulation of twenty-one point five inches. This would be the largest accumulation in the city."

The largest accumulation in the city is in Queens! Brian lives in Fresh Meadows, which is in Queens! He leaps up from his bed and presses his face against the window so that he can see the largest accumulation of snow in the city. Outside, the wind blows hard and hissy like a snake down the street as it picks up the snow from one place and puts it down in another. The largest accumulation in the city, right outside his window.

"Brian," his father suddenly calls from downstairs.

"Yes," Brian answers, turning away from the window.

"Brian," his father calls again, a little louder and a little more annoyed this time.

"Yes," Brian answers a little louder.

"Brian!" his father screams. "Will you come here this goddamn minute! If I have told you once, I've told you a thousand times to come when I call you!"

Brian leaves his room and heads down the hallway. At the top of the stairs, he looks down at his father, who is looking up at him from the bottom of the staircase.

"I need you to help me shovel the driveway," his father says sternly, a black wool hat pulled down to the top of his eyebrows so that all Brian can see of his face are two angry eyes, a nose, and a thick dark moustache above an unsmiling face. "Get your snow clothes on and come outside. And don't take too long. We've only got a few hours of light left."

Wearing thick brown knit gloves, a red bubble down jacket, a green and white wool hat drawn down tightly over his ears, and navy blue nylon snow pants tucked into brown and yellow rubber boots, Brian pushes open the rusting aluminum basement door and steps into a world of snow, glorious snow. The largest accumulation in New York City! Brian loves the cold, sharp smell of the snow, and breathes in extra hard so that he can taste it in his mouth. Then the wind gusts and blows snow into his open mouth. He turns his face away from the wind.

"Is that you?" his father impatiently asks from somewhere beyond the wind.

Brian follows his father's voice down a short, shoveled concrete path that leads to the garage. He stops at the wide entrance and looks inside. The dingy gray walls are lined with shelves packed to overflowing with boxes and dirty plastic containers that are themselves packed to overflowing with screwdrivers and wrenches and ratchets and hammers and drills and saws and files and other assorted tools and gadgets, and strange cans filled with strange liquids that burn the eyes and nose when they are opened up and poured into different parts of the car. In the midst of this repairman's bunker, Brian's father, Murry, stands with his back to the garage entrance, fiddling at a work table with some unseen contraption.

"Pick up a shovel and get to work," he commands without turning around. "Damn it," he curses as something drops to the concrete floor with a ping.

Two metal shovels—one large and covered with rust, the other smaller and still mostly its original silver—lean against the wall near the garage entrance between an automobile radiator and a decaying cardboard box filled with used nails. Brian picks up the silver shovel—his shovel. He doesn't have to be told what to do because he has shoveled snow before. He walks slowly out into the driveway, his boots crunching with each step he takes in the new white snow that comes up over his knees in several places. He picks a particularly deep spot, lifts the shovel high in the air and jams it down into the snow. The shovel goes in easily because the snow is soft. Brian lifts the shovel, but that is not easy because there is now a lot of snow on his shovel and just then there is big gust of wind which causes him to lose his balance, blowing him and the shovel full of snow to the ground.

Murry turns around and sees his son sitting on his ass in the snow. "Damn," he curses. Springing into action as quickly as a man with a bad back can, he picks up the large rusty shovel and lumbers out into the deep snow, the shovel blade held chest level like a weapon about to be used in battle.

"What the hell are you doing?" he yells as he reaches his fallen son. "This is a serious snowstorm, and you've got to shovel the right way, otherwise I'll never get this driveway cleared before it gets dark outside. I'll show you how to do it. Watch me closely."

Brian stands up and watches his father lift the rusted shovel so that the end of its blade is level with the side of his face. Murry then swings both his arms back violently so that the shovel's handle and his left elbow are even with his left shoulder. Bending his legs and back in an exaggerated manner so that his body is all angles and curves, Murry drives the shovel into the ground with the kind of force that must be associated with a loud grunt. He lifts a shovel full of snow to his chest, grunts again, and carries the shovel over to a small rectangular garden that sits alongside the driveway. With a final grunt, he dumps the snow into the garden, further burying the small pine bushes that somehow stay green even in winter. "See, you have to use your legs and arms, or else you'll hurt your back," Murry shouts across the driveway at his son. "Now let me see you do it."

Brian picks up his shovel, lifts it up to his shoulder like he just saw his father do, and drives it weakly into the snow.

"Wrong, wrong, wrong!" Murry yells so loudly that his voice carries halfway down the block. "Didn't I just show you how to do it? This time why don't you actually watch me, huh? Pay attention, for god sakes." Murry rams his shovel into the snow, then bends his legs at the knees in an even more exaggerated manner than he did the first time, as an example. "See! Legs!" he scolds his son. "Now do it correctly, okay?"

Feeling that all the windows of all the attached houses on the block are like endless pairs of eyes looking down upon him in judgment to see if he can properly shovel snow, Brian bends his legs in the same manner as his father did, then pushes his shovel into the snow as hard as he can. A spark of pain shoots through his lower back.

"Much better!" his father says approvingly.

As mid-afternoon fades into late afternoon, the grinding cacophony of metal scraping against concrete reverberates up and down the street as gently sloping driveways and ruler straight sidewalks are cleared of snow by hardworking fathers and their equally hardworking sons. A small cheer rises from among the men when a Department of Sanitation snowplow slowly rolls down the middle of the street, its large metal blade clearing a path to the avenues that bookend the block. No one can recall the last time they saw a snowplow the day after a snowstorm—usually it takes two or three days for the city to get around to plowing out Queens. Though it has been nearly ten years, no one in Fresh Meadows has forgotten John Lindsay and the blizzard of 1969. It was Mrs. Dorothy Cohen, who lived on 197th Street between 69th and 73rd Avenues before moving to Boca Raton in 1975, who famously told Lindsay to "get away, you bum," when he tried to apologize to her for the lack of snow removal. That got her quoted in the *Times*.

The good feelings quickly turn to aggravation, however, when everyone realizes that the plow has created a fresh wall of snow in front of their just cleared driveways. "Damn city still can't do anything right," Murry, who voted for Buckley in 1965 and Procaccino in 1969, mutters as he and Brian get to work on the new mountain of snow in front of their house. Half an hour later, Murry is finally able to look out upon a snow-free driveway. He experiences a moment of satisfaction, his life having been cleared of one major obstacle, though he knows there is always another obstacle ready to take its place. Damn, he has to throw salt on the driveway and the front steps or everything will freeze up overnight. Obstacles.

While Brian is watching his father take handfuls of salt out of a plastic bag and toss them on the ground, Kevin comes over. "Do you want to play in front of my house?" he asks. Kevin lives next door, and he and Brian play together because they are the same age and their parents are neighbors. When there is no snow on the ground, the two of them play in the dirt by the tree in front of Kevin's house with their G.I. Joe and Action Jackson dolls, pretending that G.I. Joe and Action Jackson are on a top-secret mission to attack enemy headquarters, which is located inside the fire hydrant next to the tree.

"Daddy, can I play with Kevin in front of his house?"

"For a little while. Don't go too far, it's going to get dark soon."

Kevin and Brian sit down on the ground in front of Kevin's house where the dirt would be if it weren't covered in snow today. The boys decide, and no one knows who makes the decision, to build a city in the snow. They start digging their gloved hands into the snow, shaping the formless particles of water and ice into the objects of a great city. Kevin makes an Empire State Building out of snow. Brian makes a World Trade Center out of snow. Kevin tops that, making a Statue of Liberty out of snow.

While the boys are building their city, their fathers stand together on the cleared sidewalk, talking. Actually, Murry does the talking while Mort Silver, Kevin's father, does the listening.

"It's just gotten worse over the years," Murry says excitedly, looking up at the three double windows—one set on the first floor, two on the second—of his brick-face row house, which is attached and identical to Mort Silver's house next door, which is attached and identical to the house next door to it, which are attached and identical to the rest of the houses on the block, and the next block, and the block after that, as if someone took one house and ran it through a mimeograph machine in order to create a neighborhood. Though the blocks of identical houses with their identical seven-step porches that lead to identical metal-screen doors with identical adjustable glass slats have confused more than one visitor to the neighborhood—"Your house is on 196th *Place*? How is that different from 196th *Street*? The houses all look the same!"—the architectural uniformity of Fresh Meadows is a great comfort to Murry who, like a cat, finds reason in the repetition of routine.

"We in Queens pay the highest taxes in the city, and get the worst service in return," he declares angrily, his face scrunched up like he just sucked a lemon. "You can thank your liberal Manhattan politicians for that." He looks up past his house and into the gray sky, and puts his gloved hands together in mock prayer. "Thank you, Abe Beame. Thank you, Ed Koch."

Mort Silver nods his head up and down at regular, rehearsed intervals, not saying a word in agreement nor disagreement, a pinched smile frozen on his face. Raised on the Lower East Side back when it was a hothouse of true radical thought and not a home to drug-addicted punks, Mort Silver's parents, Sylvia and Samuel—first-generation Jews from Poland and Russia respectively, as well as committed and admitted socialists—instilled in their only son an appreciation for the plight of the underprivileged and disadvantaged, as well as an understanding of how big business is a friend to no one but big business. "We peasants, artisans, and others, enrolled among the sons of toil, let's claim the earth henceforth for brothers, and drive the indolent from the soil," Samuel would slurringly sing, sitting in his easy chair after dinner, his son and an empty six-pack of Rheingold at his feet.

From his adolescence through his undergraduate years at City College, where he studied Marx and Engels and the exploitation of the proletariat, Mort Silver believed what his parents believed about the condition of the world. But then he graduated from college and got a job with the New York City Department of Housing, met and married Helen Fleckman, a sensible girl from Coney Island who didn't know anything about and didn't care to know anything about the bourgeois or the indolent, had a son named Kevin, bought a house in a nice neighborhood called Fresh Meadows and was mugged by a gang of black teenagers on the subway ride to work one day. As a result of these "changing realities of the world," as he calls them, Mort Silver's political and social views shifted a bit toward the middle. Maybe big business wasn't all bad, as there is nothing wrong with trying to earn a few bucks, you know, for your family. And while equality of the races might be fine for drunken old socialists sitting in their easy chairs, perspectives shift when a gang of *schvartzes* are holding a knife to your throat on the E train.

Still, no matter how much reality has changed, Mort Silver is and always will be the son of his parents. So while he can see the logic in what Murry is saying, or at least how Murry can see the logic in what Murry is saying, Mort Silver knows that he will never himself think the way Murry thinks, despite the rise in crime in New York over the past two decades.

"And of course, you can also thank the liberals for turning this city over to the *schvartzes*," Murry continues, his gaze now focused on his brown Pontiac, parked in front of his house and buried in snow, which he'll have to clear off if he wants to get to work tomorrow. Obstacles. "Because they say we need to have integration and equality, I have to have two locks on my front door, as well as an alarm." For once, Mort Silver nods in agreement, as he too has two locks on his front door, and an alarm.

"Well, at least this neighborhood has taken steps to keep the riffraff out." Murry's loud voice lowers to a whisper. "You know Larry Levin, from down the block? He has a friend who works at the Fresh Meadows rental office who told Larry that they've been redlining the *schvartzes*."

Mort Silver has heard stories of real estate agents drawing red lines on the applications of black people who want to buy houses in white neighborhoods, but he never thought that the stories were actually true. And that it was happening in his neighborhood. Changing realities of the world.

All the boys need to do to finish their city in the snow is to build a Holland Tunnel. Last summer, Brian drove through the Holland Tunnel with his mommy and daddy to visit mommy and daddy's friends in New Jersey, and he discovered that without a Holland Tunnel, you can't get in or out of the city, so they have to build a Holland Tunnel so that people can get in and out of their city in the snow.

"Now I'm sure that the liberals would be marching up and down 73rd Avenue if they heard about what was going on," Murry says, "but as my mother used to say, people should know their place in the world and stay where they belong."

The Holland Tunnel is complete! Brian and Kevin stand up so that they can examine their creation. To an adult passerby, it might look like nothing more than a few odd shapes in the snow, perhaps a small drift that the wind made. But to the imagination of two young boys, it is a living and breathing city, filled with cars and buses and bridges and people and an Empire State Building and a World Trade Center and a Statue of Liberty and a Holland Tunnel.

"I'm sure you remember how it was when we were kids," Murry says, his voice involuntarily returning to its usual excessive volume. "You could leave your door unlocked at night because some *schvartze* wasn't going to break in and steal everything. Back then, everybody knew their place. The *schvartzes* stayed up in Harlem, the PRs stayed in Puerto Rico. I don't think it's a coincidence that we didn't have problems with crime and drugs." He pauses for a moment to watch Brian and Kevin play in the snow. "I feel bad for the boys, having to grow up in today's screwed up world. They'll never know how wonderful it was to be young back when we were young, right?"

It was the day after the blizzard of 1947, and his father had built a snow fort in the backyard. Murry stood there in wonder, gazing upon the white walls made of snow. "Go inside," his mother said, her eyes bright and alive, not filled with anger or exhaustion or, as they would be in the hospital at the end, death. "It's a lot of fun. Watch me." She got down on her hands and knees and crawled in through the small opening. Murry got down on the ground and followed her in. "You two are both nuts," his father said, laughing. Once he was inside that world of white with her, Murry knew that nothing could hurt him.

"Hey, I've got an idea," Murry says, interrupting himself. "Brian and Kevin, come here."

The boys get up from the ground and walk over to where their fathers are standing.

"Do you two know what a snow fort is?" Murry asks the boys.

A snow fort? They don't know. They want to know.

"Because Mort and I have been talking, and we think it is about time you boys saw what a good, old-fashioned snow fort looks like, built by two boys who grew up in old New York."

Old New York boy Mort Silver doesn't recall there being any snow forts on Delancey Street.

Brian and Kevin stand together and watch as first Murry, and then eventually and reluctantly, Mort, begin to shovel the pile of snow in front of Brian's house. The hot, hard-working breath of the two men is visible in the cold winter air as shovelful by shovelful, the mass of shapeless snow is slowly transformed into a shallow pit, surrounded by a waist-high wall.

As Mort shovels out an entranceway on the side of the wall facing the sidewalk, Murry walks down the driveway and disappears into his garage. He emerges with a large canvas tarp in his arms, which he places over the top.

"Here it is boys, an old-fashioned New York City snow fort!"

Kevin and Brian get down on the ground, crawl quickly through the entrance and find themselves encased inside a womb of snow. They laugh and scream with delight, pressing their hands along the white walls, pretending that they are inside a real fort in the old West, surrounded by Indians, like on *F-Troop* or *The Lone Ranger*.

Their joyous squeals are interrupted by the thump of a shovel banging on the canvas roof. "I'm coming in," a deep voice declares. They are under attack! "Defend the fort against all interlopers," Brian yells because he heard the word interlopers on TV once and he knows it means that you are under attack.

"Here I come!" the voice says again. Suddenly, the roof of the fort comes off. Both boys scream in joyful terror. "Defend the fort against all interlopers!" Brian shouts as his father's grinning face, half-silhouetted by the streetlight which has just popped on as the last of the afternoon light dissolves into the coming night, looks down at him.

"I'm coming in, Bri," he says.

Brian screams a very happy scream. He loves his daddy very much right now. But he must also repel the interloper. Picking up a fistful of snow in his hand, he shouts, "Defend the fort against all interlopers," again and smashes the snow into his father's face.

It is not a lot of snow, no more than what the hand of a child can hold, but to Murry, it feels like the time he was sucker punched at work by that crazy *schvartze*, Griffin. He didn't see it coming, and then there was blood in his mouth and his jaw hurt for a week.

"Goddamn it!" Murry yells, and before he realizes what he is doing, his gloved left hand is slapping Brian hard across the cheek. The unexpected assault sends Brian tumbling backward into the wall of the snow fort. A chunk of snow falls onto his hat and face.

The sound of children's laughter stops. Kevin tries to get as far away from Murry as he can, but there is no way out of the snow fort, so he cowers in the corner, his back against the wall of snow.

Mort Silver takes a few steps back. He was six or seven, and it was dark. His father was in the room. At least he thinks it was his father—he remembers the smell of beer. From out of the darkness came a hand, slapping him across the face. Was it real, or was it a dream? It's been such a long time.

Murry stands alone. He should tell his son he's sorry, he knows that; he snapped, people get angry, that's life. Yes, that's life in this terrible world: a world of angry *schvartzes* and crazy hippies and women burning their bras in the street. That is why he has worked two jobs for the past five years, so that he could save up enough money to buy his family a house in a nice, safe neighborhood like Fresh Meadows, a neighborhood of green grass and park benches and decent, honest people who look out for one another. A neighborhood of order. A neighborhood where

Brian will have a chance to have a normal childhood, protected from the senseless violence of a world gone wrong. Yes, Brian, I'm sorry. But, if you are going to survive in today's world, where everyone feels that "theys are entitled" to whatever the fuck they want, then I, as your father, have to teach you the difference between what is right and what is wrong, no matter the cost. I have to make a hard adult out of a soft child. Maybe you won't understand now, but one day, when you have children of your own, and the two of us are sitting together in the backyard, father and son drinking a beer on a warm summer night, you'll turn to me and say, "Thanks, dad, thanks for everything."

"You could break someone's jaw doing that," Murry yells. "Never do that again. You hear me? Never!"

Brian looks up into his father's eyes, but the brightness of the streetlight against the dark sky has obliterated any details of his face. Staring into the blinding darkness, Brian wishes that winter would suddenly turn to summer and melt the snow fort away forever, and his father along with it. A few tears roll down his cheeks.

Murry looks down at his son, but it is now too dark for him to see anything.

Tired fathers and tired sons put their shovels away in silent garages, then head inside their warm homes, careful to turn on the porch light to keep away the undesirable elements that emerge with the night. Soon, everyone is enjoying a well-earned meal, followed by a Saturday night in front of the television watching Archie, Edith, Mary, Bob, and Carol.

The snow has moved completely out to sea. The clear, black sky over New York City is now painted with white stars. It is hard to see the stars in Manhattan, their ancient brightness obscured by the great height and light of the Empire State Building and the World Trade Center and the other tall buildings that separate sky from earth, but in the outlying suburban areas of the city, in neighborhoods like Fresh Meadows, where life is slower and structures smaller, they glow diaphanously.

Four Poems

Juanita Torrence-Thompson

Life in Queens—A Sestina

Manhattan is a memory; our future, Queens
where our young son can climb our swaying trees
romp through emerald grass with new friends
smell rainbow-dipped flowers in a rainbow-
sprayed borough, with stability and community,
where druggist, cleaners, mail carriers know us.

Europeans, Africans, North and South Americans live near
   us
in our hometown-cosmopolitan Queens.
Friendly Asians, W.I., Central Americans & more create
   communities
with cultures alive and appealing. We trim our trees,
mow our lawns, chat with our rainbow
connection which mirrors the world. Friends

visit and are amazed at our melting pot. Friends
enjoy picnics at Flushing Meadow Park with us,
NY Philharmonic Concerts at Cunningham Park, where
   rainbows
dwell in the sky and perch upon park lawns in Queens.
Cherry blossoms, forsythias and roses blend with jade trees,

adding delicate scents to Cape Cods and Tudor
    communities.

Queens Museum and Colden Center are community
landmarks to frequent with family and friends.
Queens Theatre erupts with vitality amid emerald trees
with concerts by Ugandan children and more to excite us.
Hall of Science for budding scientists and curious. In
    Queens
there's so much to do, or relax and stare at a rainbow
or invite black, white, red, yellow and brown for rainbow
gatherings. Play a little music for your community
of neighbors. A little Billy Joel, Lena, Cyndi Lauper with
    Queens
ties, or toss on a bit of Sinatra and Ella for friends
to enjoy. They know thoughtful or buoyant talk abounds
    with us.
They leave admiring the breeze and the trees.

Generations can be traced on family trees.
UN diplomats bring families, adding to the rainbow.
We've basked in the plethora of education available to us
and those who live and travel to our community.
La Guardia and JFK make travel easier with family and
    friends.
When visitors come to explore heterogeneous Queens

we show our community has tennis, baseball, concerts
    under trees
Botanical Gardens of rainbow-dipped bulbs for them and
    us,
but mostly amiable families and friends. That's Queens.

We'll Always Have Queens Borough Bridge

Layer upon layer
Like gray strawberry shortcake
Your levels thrust into the skyline
Linking Queens to Manhattan

Buses and trucks roll
past your juxtaposed steel beams
People glide by in cars
To work, school, travel or play

You are taken for granted
—you metallic wonder—
We're sure you'll always be there
—like Mount Everest—
despite erosion, rain, sleet, fog, snow

We assume you'll be there
Jutting skyward
Like a giant mythological behemoth
And, like in fairy tales or Monopoly,
You'll always be a free passage,
Forever interlocking our majestic boroughs

As we travel to our destinations
In our separate but intermingled lives
Meshing into one great tree
With quintuplet borough branches

Woman Walking in Queens

She crosses Main Street
wearing a black knit suit
with black and gold zigzagged top,
complementing her
Hershey bar skin.

Her smartly coiffed ebony hair
frames her tense face. Her eyes
glisten with intelligence.

She limps slightly,
using a portable folding chair
to steady her gait.
There is dignity in her bearing.

Perhaps she is someone's mother,
grandmother, sister or aunt.
Maybe she's a retired teacher
who taught in Watts, Jamaica,
or the silk stocking district.

Perhaps she's a retired nurse
or social worker dedicated to
helping the indigent.
Or she could've been a biochemist
on the verge of a scientific breakthrough
when forced to retire.

Maybe she walked with Dr. Martin Luther King
or sat on the bus after Rosa Parks
Maybe she helped Shirley Chisolm
or Justice Thurgood Marshall
Or perhaps she was a lawyer and helped
Barbara Jordan with the Southern Poverty Law Center
          This determined woman remains
an enigma as the light changes to green
and I turn the corner,
my mind jammed with possibilities.

Fowl Ball in New York

While preparing breakfast, she spotted from her kitchen window three white chickens parading near her back yard apple tree. She blinked in disbelief. The only chickens she'd seen in Queens lay supine and fresh in plastic at Waldbaum's super market.

She called her husband, Harry, to look at the brazen chickens eating her small plot of grass. Did chickens eat grass? She wondered. Harry calmly shooed them away.

The woman telephoned her neighbor from Trinidad who said, "That's old news! They come to my yard and eat my pepper plants. I took their picture since I'd never seen a chicken in the city. There used to be four but the owner down the road ate one. He's a Russian policeman—about 26. He lets them roam the streets. He keeps pet pigeons. People complained, but nothing happened."

The woman thanked her friend then scrambled three eggs and thought, I don't suppose those chickens laid these.

A Queens Necropolis: The Burial and Building of New York

Marc Landas

Give me your tired, your poor,
Your huddled masses yearning to breathe free,
The wretched refuse of your teeming shore.
Send these, the homeless, tempest-tossed to me,
I lift my lamp beside the golden door!

—"The New Colossus" by Emma Lazarus

From different points within First Calvary Cemetery, an unfocused and imaginative gaze can trace the outlines of a lost time. The southernmost tip of the cemetery gates brings you within yards of Newtown Creek, a weary and unused estuary that acts as a natural divide between Brooklyn and Queens. From the corners of your eyes, the curve of nearby buildings and streets parallels the creek until it seeps into the sweeping East River currents. In the distance looms Manhattan—unavoidable and inevitable in its grandeur.

More than a century and half has passed since the connecting rivers formed a network of death between the city and the cemeteries in Queens. Calvary Cemetery had its own ferry service that was often crammed with carriages. Every day, a boat set out from the 23rd Street Pier in Manhattan and traversed the East River, laboring against swirling currents, carrying America's newest inhabitants to their final resting place. Standing upright like a mast, the ship's navigator bore sole responsibility for the safe transport of the deceased from the land of the living to, in essence, a city of the dead. With great care, they would drift toward the Newtown Creek's gaping mouth while Manhattan's canyons of buildings and forests of steeples receded in the background.

Today, ferries have been supplanted by bridges and tunnels, the East River is as desolate as it is deserted, and Newtown Creek—polluted and toxic—has joined the ranks of the borough's dead. Between cemetery headstones and monuments, blades of grass wilt and disintegrate where feet have trod paths; meanwhile, statues sink into the ground a few more millimeters every year. New York City bustles just outside the gates and fences surrounding the grounds and can be heard from just about anywhere within the cemetery, even if merely as an ever-present hum. The days of quiet Queens countrysides have vanished; in their wake, a cacophony of artificial sounds percolate from asphalt roadways.

The shifting sounds of New York are not limited to the inanimate barks and warbles of trembling steel. The city is a composite of its inhabitants. It reflects their dreams and fears, their influences and influence, and speaks of the shared metropolitan experiences that transform strangers into neighbors. And nothing offers a better running record of its citizens than the burial grounds dotting the city because no amount of libraries or archives can match the intimacy of a single gravestone.

Since the earliest days of Dutch colonial rule, the fate of New York's outer borough has always been tied to that of "the city," where the seat of the local government resided since 1624. The title to the land that came to be known as Queens was acquired from the Metoac in 1639 and soon after, the villages of Hempstead (1643), Gravesend (1645), Jamaica (1655), and Newtown (1656) were established. And while the land belonged to the Netherlands, English immigrants constituted a majority on Long Island. Willing to swear a conditional allegiance to the Dutch government, they had descended from New England in search of the religious freedom they had been denied by the Puritans, who themselves had fled England in the hopes of worshiping without harassment. Already, three recurring themes in Queens' history emerge: its subservience to the Manhattan elite, its role as a repository for secondary citizens, and its prominence as a place of religious tolerance, predating the establishment of the English colony of Pennsylvania by almost forty years.

From the outset, the relationship between the indigenous tribes on Long Island and the European newcomers had been a cooperative one. However, on occasion, it was fraught with intermittent tensions, misunderstandings, and conflict. Eventually, the minor skirmishes broke out into all-out war in 1643; New Amsterdam's governor, Willem Kieft, essentially orchestrated conflict when, after a series of questionable incidents between natives and townsfolk, he mobilized 129 Dutch soldiers for an attack. On the evening of Feb. 23, 1643, they descended on an unsuspecting village while the villagers slept and proceeded to massacre indiscriminately. A Dutch colonist wrote in his journal:

> Infants were torn from their mothers' breasts, and hacked to pieces in the presence of their parents, and pieces thrown into the fire and in the water, and other sucklings, being bound to small boards, were cut, stuck, and pierced, and miserably massacred in a manner to move a heart of stone. Some were thrown into the river, and when the fathers and mothers endeavored to save them, the soldiers would not let them come on land but made both parents and children drown.[1]

For the first time in decades, the Algonquin tribes of the region were united thanks to a common enemy. Their response was swift and brutal. One account summarized the devastation inflicted on Long Island communities:

> Long Island is destitute of inhabitants and stock, except a few insignificant places over against the Main, which are about to be abandoned. The English have not escaped. They too, except one place, are all murdered and burnt by the Indians.[2]

And while a peace treaty was eventually negotiated with the Long Island tribes, New Amsterdam fell victim to another hostile population: the English.

Unfortunately for the Dutch, by the mid-1650s, they were sandwiched between the English colonies of Maryland to the south and Connecticut to the north—a precarious position that eventually led to the concession of New Amsterdam and its surrounding area to the English in 1664, after the Anglo-Dutch Wars in Europe. New Amsterdam was renamed New York, in honor of the Duke of York, who would eventually rise to the throne as James II. As was the custom, the conquering culture incorporated the existing one, rather than expelling them completely. It resulted in a multicultural community that would presage the city's immigrant future.

Under the English, the area that comprises present-day Queens consisted mainly of farms, wilderness, and stretches of open space, broken up by intermittent hamlets of commerce centered in the small towns spread throughout Long Island. The area's development during the eighteenth and early nineteenth centuries faltered several times due to sporadic efforts at infrastructure development. A sustained attempt at building roads never materialized and without them, transporting goods from Long Island agricultural districts to Manhattan proved unwieldy. Meanwhile, the population of Queens continued its steady ascent, placing still further stress on the limited means of travel—horse or wagon.

Burials generally took place in churchyards or on private plots, often belonging to farm owners. One example of a private farm that served dual purposes was the Alsop farm, which also doubled as a Protestant burial ground. Another graveyard still in existence sits outside the Dutch Reformed Church in Elmhurst. Public cemeteries were virtually nonexistent.

At the same time, Manhattan and Brooklyn populations skyrocketed and land development could not expand fast enough to keep pace, resulting in overcrowded areas. The larger populations also meant more deaths. According to the customs of the time, decomposing bodies were often buried in proximity to where the deceased lived. With limited space available, urban burials became a point of contention among citizens of Manhattan and Brooklyn.

When the Revolutionary War erupted, New Yorkers were sucked into the hostilities with the rest of the colonies. With the exception of Newtown, they sympathized with the Tories and the area became such a stronghold for British troops that possession of the city was barely contested. In essence, all of Long Island, including Brooklyn and Queens, became one giant staging point for British soldiers.

As the dead mounted on both sides, adequate burials became a rarity. Citizens complained of the "pestilential vapors" that emanated from graveyards that had reached their limit. Trinity Church in Manhattan was so overrun one winter that soldiers were buried in shallow graves in the frozen ground. When the ground began to thaw, the rate of decomposition quickened, releasing horrific odors from the soil. The stench persisted for at least another fifty years. By 1822, one report bemoaned the fact that Trinity Church's modest yards contained nearly 125,000 bodies, the most recent of which were buried a meager eighteen inches below ground. Eventually, fifty-two casks of lime powder were spread over every inch of the yard in the hopes of slowing the putrid stench's march.

Foul smells from decomposing bodies meant more than just a source of inconvenience. At the time, medical experts believed that death smells potentially carried disease contagions. According to contemporary theories of spontaneous generation, life could potentially take form from inanimate or unrelated substances. In the case of the buried corpses, it was likely believed that the decaying bodies gave rise to an infinite number of diseases due to their fetid nature.

During the course of its early history, New York suffered several major outbreaks of yellow fever and cholera. The former first appeared in 1668 and continued to strike with surprising frequency until the late nineteenth century. The latter took a while longer, reaching North America in 1832 and breaking out in New York City on June 26 of that year; it peaked at one hundred deaths per day during July, and finally abated in December. More than 3,500 people died in the city, many in the lower-class neighborhoods, particularly Five Points. Another 80,000 people, one-third of the population, are said to have fled the city during the epidemic.

After the 1832 outbreak of cholera, the city of New York took action. On April 27, 1847, the New York State Legislature passed the Rural Cemetery Act, which authorized commercial burial grounds in "rural" parts of New York state. In order to encourage developers, the law stipulated that nonprofit entities were allowed to establish cemeteries on rural lands and sell burial plots. Any land used in that fashion would be exempted from property taxation. The sole limitation imposed on potential cemetery owners was that the total area of each plot could not be any more than 250 acres.

At the time, Queens was still an underdeveloped network of farms and isolated towns existing on the outskirts of the rapidly urbanizing cities of New York and Brooklyn. It clearly met the criteria for burials as well as their needs. With two of the largest populated cities in the United States as its neighbors, Queens was the logical choice of a location for cemeteries and had little say in the matter. Land developers and churches agreed. A rush to buy up property in Queens ensued and St. Patrick's Cathedral, its trustees, and the Archdiocese of New York bought farmland in Newtown belonging to the Alsop family, including the Protestant graves already present. Calvary Cemetery was born.

Burying the dead brings with it a degree of artifice. There is nothing natural or intuitive about placing a body in the ground or on a pyre. From a physical standpoint, the difference between burial and cremation is only a matter of disposal. It is also a question of pragmatism; something needs to be done with the deceased, particularly for non-nomadic societies who are tied to their location. Yet, it is the artifice that allows the act of burying a loved one to be fraught with significance. We make it matter. How and where they are buried communicates respect and caring. Whether for our own benefit or not, we believe that the deceased retain a degree of earthly consciousness, which is why we lay flowers on graves, maintain the area where they are buried, and sometimes speak to their marble-etched names. Their final resting place represents a final, tangible link to the deceased. During the nineteenth century, Europe and America experienced a movement that glorified the construction of cemeteries, and many sought to transform them into lush experiences for visitors. Landscape designers, architects, and development companies insisted on moving past the simple churchyard burial. They designed parks that were not only meant to be the final resting places for the deceased but also as public spaces people could visit on weekends. Visitors could stroll through weaving paths, sit under the shade of birch and oak trees, or admire the wildlife congregating around a lily pond. Père Lachaise Cemetery in Paris represented the first of the grand gestures to the dead; built in 1804 under the rule of Napoleon Bonaparte, the rural cemetery was the result of a decree banning cemeteries within Parisian city walls. Soon after, a number of elaborate cemeteries were built in London (collectively known as the Magnificent Seven) as well as in America (such as Mount Auburn Cemetery near Boston). The first cemetery in the tri-state area was Green-Wood Cemetery in Brooklyn, founded in 1838. Calvary Cemetery belonged to this tradition.

In its current incarnation, Calvary Cemetery consists of four distinct sections collectively known as New Calvary Cemetery. Three plots run concurrently from north to south while the fourth sits separate from her sisters. Third Calvary, aka St. Sebastian Division, is bounded by the massive Queens Boulevard to the north and the Brooklyn-Queens Expressway to the south. Second Calvary, aka St. Agnes Division, is bounded by the BQE on its northern border and the Long Island Expressway on the opposite end. Fourth Calvary, aka St. Domitilla Division, is the only one of the three "new" cemeteries not surrounded by major roadways on two sides. Though it borders the LIE on its northern end, the modest two-lane road of 55th Street occupies the other end. Meanwhile, the BQE and the LIE separates the oldest and largest section, First Calvary, aka St. Calixtus Division, from the others. Together, they form the largest cemetery in the United States, and one of the oldest. Suffice to say, it is also one of the most beautiful.

As is the case with most modern cemeteries, the linear arrangement of burial plots and markers flows across the manicured grass, granite, marble, and limestone ripples on an ocean of green. Roads, paths, and walkways offer pedestrians and motorists access to every corner of the cemetery, while gaps between gravestones offer more intimate routes. Mausoleums and trees line both sides of roads creating a neighborhood of the dead. Ivy-covered vaults penetrate hillsides. Crosses sweep into the horizon while angels mourn and sing and struggle and protect, issuing proclamations to visitors and residents alike. Individual gravestones combine the poetry of the names with subtle interplays etchings and bas-relief sculptures. At the heart of Old Calvary, atop a crowded hill, sits a magnificent, domed structure—more cathedral than mausoleum—that imposes its solemnity on its surroundings.

Calvary Cemetery is a Catholic burial ground belonging to the Archdiocese of New York and maintained by St. Patrick's Cathedral's Board of Trustees. When the building now known as Old St. Patrick's Cathedral on Spring and Mott Streets was first erected, Old World tensions plagued New York. The Protestant majority stood in constant opposition to the miniscule but growing Catholic minority and the animosity often spiraled into violence, both physical and symbolic. Skirmishes and riots were complemented by the desecration of church walls and parishoners' graves.

During the early 1800s, the flood of Irish Catholic migrants that inundated the East Coast deposited a sizable population in Manhattan and Queens, most notably in Astoria, some parts of Newtown, and Jamaica, to a lesser degree. For the next century and a half, they called those neighborhoods their home. However, the greatest portion ended up in the Lower East Side, particularly the area known as Five Points. By the 1840s, the wave of Irish immigrants turned into a flood as a result of the Great Irish Famine of 1845, brought on by an epidemic of potato blight across Ireland. Millions of people set out on the perilous journey across the Atlantic, hoping to escape the desperation of their homeland and find food in a new land. Many died on the trip over, so many that the ships were nicknamed "coffin ships." By this time, the Irish made up half of the total number of immigrants entering the United States, and as they settled into their communities—often the preexisting ones settled by the initial wave—small communities exploded into large ones.

Even without religious tensions, conflict between immigrant groups and established groups is natural, especially when they vie for the same jobs. The gradual reshuffling of pecking orders can often be painful. It was only a matter of time until Old World tensions surfaced and combined with New World characteristics. Specifically, the animosity fostered by centuries-old religious conflicts was inflamed by newer anti-immigrant sentiments. Every day, Irish Catholics struggled not only to adjust to a new culture, but also to survive repeated attacks by the anti-Catholic majority that often packaged their hatred in the guise of patriotism. In Philadelphia, the so-called Nativist Riots saw dozens of Irishmen killed and two Catholic churches burned to the ground. Officials in New York City worried that the nativist movement would next target the city's

Catholic churches. It was under these circumstances that the Ancient Order of Hibernians formed. It was a mobile Irish army that protected Irish interests in the heart of New York City.

A Catholic church in the middle of a Protestant city, St. Patrick's was the seat of the Bishop of New York and served as protector of Catholic souls, particularly the Irish immigrant population in what is now the Lower East Side. The church was dedicated on May 14, 1815. At the time, it towered over surrounding structures, with its inner vault stretching eighty-five feet at its highest point and its steeple reaching almost one hundred. Until the opening of the larger cathedral uptown on Fifth Avenue, it was the seat of the Archdiocese of New York and home to the first Archbishop of New York, Bishop Luke Concanen, in 1808.

From the day it opened its doors, the parish had its share of tumult. After a mob surrounded the cathedral and tried to burn it down, the church constructed thick, ten-foot tall brick walls around the entire property in 1835. It was probably for the better, since the public's attitudes toward the Irish deteriorated after the nativist movement took shape across the eastern seaboard. Things eventually came to a head when an angry mob laid siege to St. Patrick's, prompting the militant Ancient Order of Hibernians to come to the rescue; the AOH then opened an office across the street from St. Patrick's as a deterrent against any further aggressions. From that day forward, the association between the Irish and St. Patrick's would remain intertwined until the late twentieth century; the relationship is commemorated with a plaque by the entrance doors. In exchange for the stewardship of the AOH on the earth, St. Patrick's tended to their afterlife. It was in this role that the trustees of St. Patrick's Cathedral created a cemetery that was designed to address the severe overcrowding of the two graveyards that straddle the northern and southern ends of the building.

As a besieged population living in New York, Catholics needed to maintain solidarity, and Calvary Cemetery symbolized that notion. In that sense, St. Patrick's fulfilled its role as being spiritual caretakers of its New York flock. Take a trip to the cemetery and it would be easy to say that they not only fulfilled expectation, but surpassed it; Calvary Cemetery is both a functional cemetery and a beautiful one. And therein lies the significance of Calvary Cemetery. The aesthetics of the landscaping is not beauty for the sake of beauty. Each serpentine path lined with sentinel-like marble gravestones, each rolling hill topped with a baroque mausoleum, and each brick of the majestic chapel that serves as the cemetery's spiritual locus represents an undeniable effort to protect and minister to the dead. By opting for something greater than a field littered with graves, the Archdiocese of New York made a statement about the Catholic community. It said, "In life and death, the Catholic Church cares for its flock." More importantly, it reinforced the solidarity needed among Catholics in the United States.

The vast majority of the oldest graves at Calvary Cemetery belong to Irish Catholics, with the exception of the forty or so Protestant plots that dated from the Alsop family's ownership. Names such as Sullivan, Johnston, and McCormack adorn headstones in First Calvary; chances are, they worshiped at St. Patrick's Cathedral on Mott Street and lived close to it. The distance from their homes meant they were also far from the world that would have desecrated their graves, given the chance. In time, the Irish in New York no longer needed to worry about desecrated graves because the American fabric absorbed them, and in the process, transformed pariahs into patriots. Their success would become symbolic of what could be achieved in America.

Newtown Creek lies still while minivans, sedans, and dirty-wheeled trucks tread overhead across the Polaski Bridge. Its currents no longer carry commerce and its waters no longer support life. It has become a natural anomaly—an estuary whose nutrients have been replaced by poisons. A thick toxic sludge lies at the river floor, the result of a century's worth of direct industrial dumping. And, as if in recognition of its ruined state, it has stopped moving from the mouth of Maspeth Creek, East Branch, and English Kills—its natural origins—into the East River. Instead, it languishes, unable to muster the vitality to move, cursed by toxic artifacts and rendered immobile by the chemicals that fueled Manhattan's movement into modernity.

For more than a century, Newtown Creek and Queens served as the industrial backbone of New York City's drive to affluence. During the 1800s, factories overran the 3.8 miles that constituted Newtown Creek's shoreline and extended deep into Long Island City, Astoria, and Woodside. The first railroad in Queens finished construction in 1836 and connected Brooklyn with Jamaica. Subsequent years witnessed further expansion of that line, first to Hicksville (now part of Nassau county) then to Suffolk station (now part of Suffolk county). A wide range of industries—including oil refineries, petrochemical plants, fertilizer and glue factories, sawmills, and lumber and coal yards—spewed waste into the air and waterway. In addition, by the middle of that century, the factories had taken to directly dumping their waste into the river, accelerating its decline. Because of its location across from Manhattan and straddling the Brooklyn-Queens border, the creek also evolved into a major waterway—first for farmers, then for the factories, and finally, by ships and ferries shuttling people, produce, and products around the city. During World War II, it was among the busiest ports in the country. By then, the die had been cast; the river's death was unavoidable.

It is said that rivers are the lifelines of the land and when rivers die, the surrounding land soon follows. With that in mind, it would not be far-fetched to consider the destruction of Newtown Creek as a serious affront to Queens' viability and her population. It is *not* an anomaly. On the contrary—the death of Newtown Creek is symbolic of a historical pattern of use, abuse, and disenfranchisement of the borough and her resources for the benefit of her more affluent neighbors. The presence of Calvary Cemetery is a relic of this attitude.

Since the establishment of New Amsterdam, the area encompassing modern-day Queens has always been a satellite of the power base. As New Amsterdam transitioned into New York and the city began its steady march northward, Queens remained agrarian and fed the voracious appetite of an expanding city. As a result, from a very early date, she developed a reputation as something of a farmland backwater. As urbanization increased in Manhattan and Brooklyn, so did the disparity between Queens and her neighbors. Her reputation as being "country" and inhabited by unsophisticated hokies in all likelihood grew.

As industrialization gripped New York, Queens served as the engine for the production of many of the goods Manhattan exported and built its wealth on. However, with an engine comes exhaust waste, and rather than being recognized for her contributions, Queens was saddled with an added reputation as being a wholly grotesque and polluted wasteland (see the reference to Astoria as the "Valley of the Ashes" in F. Scott Fitzgerald's *The Great Gatsby*). This was due to a combination of factors. Firstly, the most industrialized and polluted areas of Queens were located in the areas now known as Long Island City, Astoria, and Woodside. They were the very first parts of Queens a visitor from Manhattan and the mainland experienced. As one commentator moaned in 1908:

> The casual visitor . . . sees only the business district, in most cases that part of the borough where factories are located. Such a conglomeration of buildings entirely devoted to business of one kind or another is never and nowhere very attractive. . . . Factories turning out large quantities of goods in the price of which the cost of transportation forms an important item must be located near a railroad or within convenient distance from the shore. . . . It is therefore not

surprising that people who visit Queens . . . are disappointed and even disgusted. They shorten their stay as much as possible and go away with the impression that the borough is not fit to live in.[3]

When the Long Island Rail Road was built, the first main rail line from Manhattan into Queens ran along the banks of the already hyper-polluted Newtown Creek, which was lined with factories. For Manhattanite businessmen, Queens was a place to visit for as brief a time as possible, and in terms of residence, Queens was where people lived when they could not manage anywhere else.

During the turn of the twentieth century, Queens experienced a development boom, owing to the exploding populations in Manhattan and Brooklyn and also the creation of Greater New York City. Many of the red brick building complexes characteristic of Queens today have their roots during that era. While some parts of Queens such as Elmhurst experienced brief moments as a fashionable destination, most of the areas were marketed in a manner consistent with Queens' reputation. Advertisements for building complexes with courtyards and terraces offered "the middle-class experience" at affordable, non-middle-class prices; it allowed New York City's working class with middle-class pretensions to live their dream, even when they didn't have the money to "truly" be middle-class. In this way, Queens was built on the illusion of *achieving* the American Dream, rather than actually realizing it. This working-class character persists to this very day.

The influx of the working class was inevitably followed by immigrants. In time, the "unsophisticated" "country" label Queens' original inhabitants were pegged with was transposed into a modern-day, urban form with "farmers" being replaced by immigrants. Ultimately, it was this pervasive outlook—of Queens as country backwater—in its earlier incarnations that gave rise to Calvary Cemetery and all of Queens' cemeteries, turning the borough into an industrial park. Rather than an industrial dumping ground, Queens was considered a suitable area to discard the pestilent, decomposing bodies Manhattanites and Brooklynites refused to have in their area due to health concerns.

Yet out from the rubble, smokestacks, and decomposition that is Long Island City, Calvary Cemetery transcends its surroundings. On the periphery of Fitzgerald's Valley of the Ashes, grass-covered hills, flower beds, and avenues lined with trees take form. It has emerged as a splendid resting place for the city's immigrant and Catholic population and a testament to how strangers can become neighbors.

The demographics of Calvary Cemetery reflect the changing faces of New York City in much the same way modern-day Queens reflects the realities of a globalized world. It tells the story of immigrant New York and foretells the future that can be summed up with one word: diversity. The deeper into the twentieth century the dates range, the more diverse the languages: Italian, French, Spanish, Korean, Chinese. According to a Claritas study conducted in 2001, it is the most diverse county in the United States, of those with populations over one hundred thousand. Communities from across the globe are represented: Columbians, Irish, Italians, Ecuadorians, Dominicans, Haitians, Filipinos, Chinese, Koreans, Indian, Bangladeshi, Kenyan, Ugandan—the list goes on. Of the various ethnic groups, nearly half of Queens' population is foreign born. If we go by the 2000 Census' population count of 2,229,379, that means 1,114,690 people came to New York City in search of a promise, the way the Irish did some two centuries earlier.

Ride a train, a bus, or a car and you will discover the process already in motion. The living, breathing, and expanding Chinatown in Flushing. Little India in Jackson Heights. Haitian botanicas in Elmont. Columbian restaurants lining Roosevelt Avenue. Uzbek and Tajik restaurants and synagogues in Rego Park. And, like the Irish before them, these groups are using their growing populations to directly influence the political landscape of their adopted homes, whether it's through organizations representing their interests or elected leaders.

Queens is home to more than a half-dozen major cemeteries serving all faiths—Cedar Grove Cemetery in Flushing, Cypress Hills Cemetery straddling the Brooklyn-Queens border, Fresh Pond Crematory and Columbarium in Middle Village, Mount Zion Cemetery alongside Calvary, and Maple Grove Cemetery in Kew Gardens, to name a few. The cemeteries in Queens span the religious spectrum from Jewish to nondenominational. This is no fluke. On the contrary, the borough possesses a long tradition of tolerance and acceptance that dates back to the earliest days of its European settlement. Even as a satellite of New Amsterdam, Queens welcomed and accepted the various immigrant groups that chose to settle there. The Dutch had a history of having what could only be described as an institutional tolerance.

Every American schoolchild learns about the Pilgrims and Puritans and the persecution they suffered in Charles I's England. All they wanted was to be allowed to practice their religion without fear of being put in prison or subjected to tortures or humiliations. Unfortunately for them, the Church of England and its head, the king, refused them even the simplest respect. With no recourse but to flee the country, they formed the Plymouth Company and later, the Massachusetts Bay Colony, and embarked on what would become known as the Great Migration—or so the story goes. They constitute a major portion of the American myth, setting up the Revolution by denouncing the tyranny of England and also implying the foundation of one of America's constitutional pillars, the freedom of religion. The truth is a bit messier, thanks to group of outsiders that migrated to Dutch New Amsterdam during the seventeenth century: the English.

Their destination was not New Amsterdam proper, but rather a town in its outskirts called Vlissingen (from which the current name of Flushing derives) and, as always, Queens welcomed them with open arms and plots of land. This was no fluke. The Dutch were known throughout Europe for their religious tolerance; when religious groups sought sanctuary, they went to the Netherlands before heading to the new world. In the Dutch Republic, freedom of conscience had already been codified in the 1579 Union of Utrecht, essentially the country's constitution. Article 13 of that document stipulated that "each person shall remain free, especially in his religion, and that no one shall be persecuted or investigated because of their religion." The sentiment would reappear nearly a century later and across an ocean.

While the ideals of the Dutch Republic may have preached tolerance, the West India Company's Director-General and Governor of New Amsterdam, Petrus Stuyvesant, was anything but; he often bordered on tyrannical. The Quakers proved particularly irksome, so much so that he outright refused their presence in his colony. To drive the point home, he had a Quaker convert tortured in public. His actions only incensed the citizens of New Amsterdam. On December 27, 1657, the town clerk, a man named Edward Hart, wrote what would be known as the Flushing Remonstrance. It was signed by thirty-one other townsmen and is generally acknowledged to be the precursor for the U.S. Constitution's First Amendment provision for the freedom of religion.

While the petition failed to sway Stuyvesant—he had Hart and a few others imprisoned until they admitted their "error"—it allowed Quakers to continue meeting in Vlissingen and set the stage for John Bowne's 1663 trip to Holland, after he was arrested for harboring a Quaker. While there, Bowne pleaded his case in front of the West India Company and convinced them that Stuyvesant must allow Quakers to meet freely. The petition has been cited by historians as another predecessor to the freedom of religion promised in the First Amendment of the Constitution.

That is not to say that New York or Queens has not had its share of intolerance. But what stands out is how with time and persistence, group after group managed to rise above the prejudices pointed their way. While the ethnicity or religion might have changed, the story always proved the same in the end.

The graves in Calvary Cemetery offer a glimpse into the ascent and integration of immigrant groups in New York City. The oldest gravestones, belonging to the first waves of immigration from Ireland suggest their still tenuous situations in their new country. Fading names adorn Bible-sized slabs of white marble almost wiped clean by exposure to wind, rain, and freezing temperatures. Inscriptions of deceased infants and children, reunited with their families in death, testify to the often brutal conditions newcomers often faced, living in tenements and squalor. Many gravestones speak to the homesickness and nostalgia experienced by immigrants moving to America from across the Atlantic. They answer, once and for all, the question of origin. Ireland. Dublin. Cork. Kilkenny. Galway. Armagh. Though they died Americans, make no mistake; they were born Irish.

Calvary Cemetery accepts few new burials these days. Whatever fresh graves do materialize, with their somber brown mounds of freshly upturned dirt, belong to established family plots. For all intents and purposes, it has reached capacity, much like many of the other cemeteries in Queens. It's a far cry from the days when at least 120 bodies entered the Calvary gates each day, and longer still since forty Protestant graves made up the Alsop Family's private burial ground. Like many New York City landmarks—Ellis Island or Castle Clinton in Battery Park—its utilitarian existence will soon fade, leaving a relic that hearkens back to an era when New York City was not the center of the world and when nobody knew that strangers would come together to build Gotham.

Notes

1. Russell Shorto, *The Island at the Center of the World* (New York: Vintage Books, 2004), 124.

2. Henry Onderdonk Jr., *Queens County in Olden Times: Being a Supplement to the Several Histories Thereof* (Jamaica, NY: Charles Welling, 1865), 3.

3. George von Skal, *Illustrated History of the Borough of Queens* (New York: F. T. Smiley, 1908), 31–36.

Rockaway Sonnets

Jill Eisenstadt

The Naming

Call it Rechohahacky, lonely place
We Canarsee can foresee such sadness.
Fire, storm, shipwreck, crash, flood whitecap lace
spell out S.O.S, S.R.0.—madness.
We will disappear with the deer, cedar
and oyster. Our shell mounds beneath the Five
Towns. No shadow of our briny leader
Here Riis, Moses and Joey Ramone thrive.
Agreement in the longhouse: It's too much—
German spies and drowned Chinese illegals.
Best to trade this cursed strip to the fresh Dutch,
Leave the coming plane wreckage to seagulls.
Licked by water on three sides, the lost home
does by surviving deserve this love poem.

In the Black

Our tiny peninsula, hanging from
what they would come to call Queens was sold then
Twenty-five dollars, the deed agreed sum
Dollar more than they got for Manhattan
But honest history could never say
we'd been bilked, even here at Shinnecocke
Those who dared live between Ocean and Bay
Tilled soil salty from hurricane shock,
pirates, booze smugglers, politicos—guess
where all the city's disenfranchised went?
In the Far Rockaway of the Heart-less
Mess. There Bernie Madoff met Ruth and spent
her babysitting pay at Connolly's
Shall I compare thee to a sandy breeze?

Before the Great Sideside Fire

They came fleeing cholera and the stench
Of heated horse shit, trash, B.O. they came
on flooded, muddy roads; each pale mouth clenched
They came unable to resist the claim:
Everyone who's anyone's been seen at
Rockaway in this summer of eighteen
thirty-three. —Vanderbilts and Astors chat
on the piazza of the new Marine
Hotel. Longfellow goes in for the chic
new fad: Sea bathing. A cart and horse take
ladies in to the surf. Modest or weak
stay inside or ashore at the clam bake
They came for the air and to say they came
Burning for status, they went down in flame.

Adolescent Swell

Winter it was Rot-a-way, always last
to be shoveled out. The Pauls hid shells in
their snowballs, skitched on the ice holding fast
to the back of the Green Line Bus. Pin
Her Down and Make Her Guess What John Ate was
Spring on the Irish Rivera where
Pat checked the mushy waves all day because
Duke Kahanamoku was truly there
once and that summer we were Malibu
Queen, Rockapulco with our name in all
the papers. No Toms had to run into
fire for this, no hoarse 911 call,
or missing neighbor. By Fall, all the Mikes
who could get up and surf were zap!—heroes!

Accent Reduction

Mark Swartz

Gesturing at an expensive-looking couple across the club, I said to my date, "If you can get them into the limo with us, you'll get a big surprise." She gave me the tragic mascara over the rim of her Cabernet Sauvignon, turned on one platform heel, and sauntered up to them. As a stewardess, Margit excelled at the art of approaching strangers, making them feel comfortable, securing compliance. It didn't take long.

"Did I already tell you I love those earrings?"

"Tell *him*. He got them for me."

"What about the shoes?"

"I buy my own shoes!"

The cool and relative quiet of the street had a soothing effect. The moon and streetlights subtly changed everyone's appearance. The couple looked unpressed, probably even drunker than I'd surmised, but cheerful, almost giddy to be climbing into a car with people they'd just met. I took the passenger seat and instructed the driver to bring us to Pasquale's in Long Island City. Margit, who looked as fresh as a pint of cherry vanilla despite having been up since working the red-eye from Dallas the night before, volunteered to sit in the middle of the backseat, just as I'd asked. When I swiveled, I could look up at her skirt at long and muscled legs, but that wasn't the main point.

After we got over the 59th Street Bridge, the driver pulled between two warehouses, and stopped the car. I said, "What's going on?"

He took out a gun and murmured, "Give me the purse."

This was the chance for the boyfriend to act calm and collected. "Just don't hurt her," he said. "She's giving you the purse. It's Louis Vuitton. Real."

"And *your* wallet," the driver said to the boyfriend.

"Take the cash, here."

"I'll take the whole wallet, thank you. Even if it's not real."

I shouted at the driver: "We don't want any trouble. He's giving you cash. Look, there's . . . more than eleven hundred dollars."

Jake aimed the gun at my throat. "They can get out right now," he said. "I like them. They don't talk back." I heaved one sob, then another, quietly at first, but with violent shudders in between. "You can get out too, before you piss your pants and ruin my seat." I increased the volume.

As the two back doors opened, I refused to leave without my date, and the argument went from heated to shrill as the couple took off on foot. Margit screamed her lungs out as we drove away.

I didn't have to tell her to scream. They figured that part out themselves. It was a simple formula, quite lucrative and also very exciting for the stewardesses. They wanted a break in the monotony? Well, this was a break. And the four hundred dollars apiece didn't hurt.

My family comes from Kazakhstan. We were not the first Bukharian family in the Forest Hills, but we were the first to build a monstrosity. My father went whole hog on the home-as-castle thing. Fluted marble columns, chrome banisters, two turrets, and a widow's walk, a gilded family crest above the doorway. It was awesome. In three years we had become landed gentry of the north side of Queens Boulevard. South was for families who'd been in America two, three generations, which in Queens counts as much as coming over on the Mayflower.

"Suley, come here," my dad would call. And we'd watch the squirrels chasing each other around the copper birches he'd planted in the front yard. "You like living here?" he'd ask me.

"Sure, dad, who wouldn't?" This was not such a subtle way of reminding him that my two older brothers had fled his domineering presence for a Florida shopping mall development outfit run by our aunt.

"You're coming to work with me tomorrow," he'd say. He had a jewelry store in midtown.

"Next week, Dad, I promise."

We were global hicks, myself included. I was maybe the worst of all, with my Van Halen–worthy mullet and stone-washed 505s. It was a pure cheese sensation.

That is, until I discovered stewardesses. The airlines put them up in the high-rise condos that lined Queens Boulevard, refreshing the supply daily. Once you cleaned up (and I cleaned up nice), all you had to do was make your way over to the 5 Burros after 11 and ask one if she wanted another margarita. They were perfume-soaked sitting ducks, bored, restless, desperate for someone to listen to them about obnoxious passengers, heartless pilots, mothers who always phoned too early or too late. Guess who was all ears.

Three, four nights a week I squired a Scherri, a Teena, an Annemarie, an Ilÿsa around town, paying for the dinner, the dancing, the drinks, and the dope, and then collecting on my investment until the sun came up. An Olympic-caliber sexual athlete, I was twenty years old and in hock to a Chinese loan shark for more than eight grand.

Wu himself gave me the gun, saying there was no other way he'd ever see his money. He wore enormous glasses with a very powerful prescription, which he wiped frequently, as if a speck of dust could block his entire field of vision. When you looked him in the eyes, you couldn't even see his eyes.

I brought it to my cousin, Jake (Yakov), a chauffeur for a fancy limo company, who sometimes drove me and my date to clubs when he had to pick someone up in the city anyways.

"You want me to murder someone with this?"

"What, murder? It's not even loaded, probably."

"Suley, look," he said, releasing the cylinder to reveal six gleaming bullets.

"Okay, so it's loaded. That just makes it more realistic. I'm glad one of us knows all about guns. That's why you're keeping it up front with you. Don't let me touch that thing again."

The little game worked out fine for a couple, three months. Jake and I were making serious money, scoring as much as five thousand dollars on a lucky night. My dad had stopped inviting me to the store, and I was reaching all-new sexual highs with the stewardesses, who started referring their friends to me. No more pickups at the 5 Burros, no more hints and dodges. Just willing partners.

Jake and I were in the car at the corner of Queens Boulevard and Continental Avenue, waiting for a stewardess named Maia. He was eating Funyuns. I was trying to reach my hair stylist when another call came in.

"Suley, can I take a raincheck?"

"What do you mean?"

"Something came up. My husband. I mean my ex-husband. He got out early, and we're going to celebrate. But don't worry, my friend Rena can fill in for me."

"What did your husband do?"

"It was all a misunderstanding."

"What did they say he did?"

"Break my legs."

"*Did* he break your legs, Maia?"

"Yeah, but it was all a misunderstanding. Oh, but here's Rena."

"Hello."

"Hello, Rena, this is Suley. Nice to meet you. What time can you be at the corner of Queens Boulevard and—"

"Continental? Look out your window." I looked up as they were saying good-bye to each other and couldn't decide who was who. One was tall and dark, the other average height, with too much makeup and too little dress. When the tall dark one departed, Jake almost called it off.

"Sorry, but you cannot come with us."

"Can you put NPR on? Terry Gross is about to interview Oliver Sacks."

"Please get out of my car before I—"

"It's okay, Jake," I said. "Let's just see what's going on here first."

Rena struck a match. When the light flared, war paint accentuated the sharpness of her features. "And can we stop somewhere for sashimi beforehand? First of all, *is* there good sashimi around here? I don't do California rolls," she said, taking a long draw of a thin brown cigarette.

"It's okay, Jake," I said again, and we spun around and joined the stream of Manhattan-bound traffic.

Rena rolled down her tinted window. "I can't believe I actually used to live around here," she said. "This is actually where I would have ended up if I hadn't gone to boarding school. That would have been me over there, in the babushka with the four kids."

Jake fumed. It wasn't his family that Rena pointed to, but it might as well as have been. "You are Bukharian?" he said.

"*Shumoro dida xursand shudam,*" she responded in perfect Bukhori. I noticed that one of her two front teeth was longer than the other. "WNYC is 93.9 FM. I don't usually listen to Fresh Air, but Oliver Sacks is so brilliant. Or he's a total fraud, one or the other, but either way, I just like brains."

"Yeah, what do you like about them?" I asked.

"I love it when they malfunction. Colors become music. Ladies become hats. Hot glue tastes like chocolate pudding. Damaged brains are the most incredible thing. It's too bad they come attached to bodies. Are you guys hungry? I mean, I know we have to get to this club, but as long as we're taking the midtown tunnel, could we stop at this Japanese place on forty-eighth?"

Jake offered her the rest of his Funyuns. She declined.

In the club I ordered her a Cabernet Sauvignon, but she grabbed the waitress by the wrist and changed her order to Jägermeister.

"What do you think of *them*, Rena?" I said, pointing my chin toward a couple by the door.

"What are you, brain damaged? *My* purse cost more than hers. What else you got, Suley? Because I told Maia I'd stop by later, make sure her ex hasn't broken anything." She sipped her drink, twisting her napkin into a rope, dismissing my suggestions until I stopped making them.

"Well, what then?" I asked.

She finished her drink, kissed me sweet and herbal on the mouth and said, "I just had a brilliant idea." Jake wasn't too happy about us getting back in the car without anyone, but when Rena told him to drive us to Flushing, he obeyed. The limousine crept through Chinatown, which was only slightly less congested in the middle of the night than it was in the day, while the radio played a talk show about the new SuperCollider. Between two warehouses on Prince Street, there was a little nothing bar with some red neon Chinese characters in the window.

"This?" said Jake.

"Give us twenty minutes," answered Rena. "And don't blink at what we bring back."

Once inside, I could immediately see that she knew what she was doing. The men were in tailored suits, with cufflinks peeking out of the sleeves. The women were generally a foot taller and twenty years younger than their dates. They were exquisitely dressed and bejeweled.

They were also . . . not women. There was a small stage in the corner. One got up and belted out "Papa, Can You Hear Me?" from the movie *Yentl*.

"Ooh, a bad sign." Rena pouted, signaling to a tuxedoed waiter. "When I was ten, I begged my father for a Talmud. I don't know how I even know what one was. Eventually, he consented, and I read it obsessively all summer long. When I announced to the family that I had decided to become a rabbi, they laughed. The thing was, I knew the scripture better than our rabbi before I had my menarche. It was ridiculous that a prodigy like me would be barred from the rabbinate simply because of my sex."

Another transvestite mounted the stage and stood before an antique microphone as a saccharine string arrangement played.

> *This is Major Tom to ground control*
> *I'm stepping through the door*
> *And I'm floating in a most peculiar way*
> *And the stars look very different today*

"When I was ten, I wanted to be the first man on Mars," I said.

The singer's makeup was a work of art, pure and simple. It must have been done by a professional. Between verses she refused to smile at the onlookers, defying their adulation. Her voice was as cuddly as a gloved fist. She finished singing, and with the backing tracks still playing, she returned to her seat and planted a cold kiss on her companion's lips.

Rena patted my thigh. "I don't think your friend likes me. Excuse me if I want to listen to public radio. What does *he* do to exercise his brain, anyway? Sudoku? I tried that once and nearly had a nervous breakdown. I just don't do numbers. I'm very verbal."

"I couldn't tell."

"I read about three books a week. It doesn't matter what, as long as it's nonfiction. I can't fall asleep without reading at least an hour. Even after sex, I get up and read in the bathroom if I have to. My mind is hungry for ideas. How about them?"

I didn't recognize the singer's companion until he replaced the enormous glasses on his face.

"No way," I said. "In fact, I don't think we belong here at all."

"Do you think that's a real diamond?" She was up before I could restrain her.

And then we were all in the car. I cranked the A/C but was still sweating. Jake gripped the wheel tight enough to break off the steering column. I turned on the radio. He punched it off. Rena kept talking.

"I didn't think I'd like green tea ice cream because I don't like tea. No offense, but I'm more of a coffee person. If I don't have my three coffees before noon, I'm useless for the rest of the day. It doesn't have to be *good* coffee. I'm not one of those people. Jake, it's right around here I think. Do you think we're too early? I hate being the first one to arrive. It's almost as bad as being the last to leave."

Jake stopped the car between two dark warehouses. There was a long silence until I remembered I was supposed to say, "What's going on?" When he reached toward the glove compartment, I reacted without thinking, which is sometimes the best way. I tried to kick, but it came out as a forceful stomp. My heel was jammed against the glove compartment with Jake's hand still inside. He screamed my name before a shot rang out. At first I thought it was the gun in Jake's hand, but then he started coughing wetly.

We buried him two days later. It was a small, private ceremony. Now when people ask where my wife Rena and me met, I tell them it was at a funeral.

Koshchei the Deathless

Irina Reyn

In memory of Shimon Reyn

I.

Koshchei had freckles and scrawny arms. He had a high, hiccupy laugh. When I first transferred into this yeshiva, he was going by his real name like the rest of us, but now, on the cusp of sixth grade's finale, he had settled into the identity of "Koshchei the Deathless." For a short Russian kid barely four years off the boat like myself, he managed to carve out his own domain in the rigid social hierarchy of Gan Israel.

Inside its lime-green-painted brick walls, Gan Israel Hebrew Day School of Queens could support only a handful of cliques: Popular Americans, Loser Americans, Popular Israelis, Loser Israelis. Russian immigrants—pale, plaid, corduroy creatures and sprinkled into each grade—had to align themselves with the group of their choice. Otherwise, they would disappear.

During morning prayers, Koshchei ruled two tables away from the singing cantor. His Followers, a group of acolytes from the dustbin of the lower castes with disfiguring facial acne and detachable dental contraptions, huddled around him, hanging onto every word. He used class time to transcribe a personalized version of the Talmud, with its own idiosyncratic laws, onto a scroll of taped-together sheaves of paper. If you find a strawberry Pop Tart on the street with its wrapper still intact, be sure to bring it to Koshchei as a religious sacrifice, one law demanded.

In the playground, his throne was pressed against the school wall. From that folding chair, he could watch the dodgeball game in peace. From time to time, a Follower would whisper the score, recap a memorable moment—a particularly wily throw, an embarrassing buckling of legs.

His lunch looked no different from mine—two soggy pieces of pumpernickel bread glued together by mayonnaise, a bruised peach and a juice carton—but he ate it with the grandeur of an explorer just returned from exotic lands, bearing gifts from its natives. Like me, he never knew the right answer in Bible classes, but I imagined him privately storing up the knowledge to bring home to his parents. Unlike my parents (who could eat a ham sandwich while driving around on a Saturday), I imagined his family would treat the Jewish religion with reverence. Vaguely, I pictured candles, challah, and gold-wrapped chocolate pennies.

Teachers were confused by him. Popular Americans feared his unstable aura would rub off on them. Popular Israelis laughed at his unironic resolve. Loser Americans longed to break into the inner sanctum. Loser Israelis weaved around him, too mired in their own daily miseries to notice. I arrived in America too late, moments after identities were distributed.

More than anything else, even the health of my dedushka, I dreamed that he would invite me to the sixth-grade dance. Only Koshchei had the power to raise me from obscurity, to bring me into focus.

II.

When the bus turned onto 99th Street, I rose from my seat at the front of the bus and hauled my red backpack onto my shoulders. If I squinted my eyes, I could see the slumping form of my dedushka, standing at the bus stop, amidst young mothers, bored siblings, and Polish nannies. My mind began to drift to the surprise candy warming the inside of my dedushka's palm. Each day it was something different: a hard watermelon candy in the shape of a ring, shredded bubble gum with a benign baseball player peering out from the bag, or a slightly melted Kit-Kat that had to be devoured slowly. (First, break off one segment from the rest; next, bite the drooping chocolate around the wafer; and finally, suck on the remains until the bar collapses gently against the roof of the mouth.)

"Grandpa!" I screamed, giving an unshaven cheek a wet kiss. How innocent he appeared, lacking any conceptions of school's social hardships. I envied him, no doubt enjoying the freedom of the warm day, strolling in the park, reading a novel, blithely ignorant of life's cruelties. He hugged me and took my backpack from me, pretending to sag beneath its weight. As usual, he didn't ask about school, the two of us locked in step, communicating in silent telepathy. With my grandmother gone, Dedushka was the only observant person left in my family; only he could bridge my religious and secular worlds. But in my unspoken renditions of the time spent at school, I never told him about my raped notebook, "dirty commie" scrawled on its cover with black permanent marker. I didn't tell him that right before I got off the bus, an eighth grader had shoved my backside with her combat boot, no doubt leaving a gray dusty imprint in the middle of my skirt. I often tried to shield my grandfather from painful knowledge.

My dedushka often did the same for me. Three years ago, on one of our grocery shopping expeditions on 108th Street, I had asked him where I came from. This was a topic I had mulled over in my head for weeks, unable to work up the courage to ask my parents. We had just bought some herring and onions for the night's dinner and stepped out into the sunlight, the scent of fish sweet in the cool, spring air. It was the perfect moment to broach the issue. Dedushka seemed to consider the question carefully and finally informed me that he bought me at a famous Moscow department store that specialized in babies. He said that because it was the Soviet Union, he was forced to wait in line for four hours.

"But what if someone else bought me first?" I had asked, horrified. "How could you take that chance?"

He paused, shifting a satchel from one hand to the other, a hint of weariness clouding his eyes. "I knew no one would. You were clearly meant for me to purchase and bring back to your parents."

I imagined the long line snaking around the block, the little kids staring out of their individual jars, assessing each customer. I envisioned the pathetic scene each grandfather was faced with when he finally arrived at the head of the line, the flashes of information that would influence his choice—an upturned lip, flushed cheeks, too rapidly blinking eyes. I wondered what set me apart from the others. Perhaps I was the only one refusing to make eye contact with all the dedushkas, the first child that tried not to appear too needy.

But weeks later, when I casually mentioned Dedushka's fortuitous purchase over the dinner table, my parents froze, yellow-orange strings of *kapusta* dangling from their forks. I knew something was wrong. Although they attempted to explain their bewilderment away with stories of shorter lines and the inclusion of a complimentary loaf, they eventually broke down and explained the mysteries of conception. The next time I went for a walk with my dedushka, his white hair tousled in the budding spring wind, I could not find it in my heart to admit that I knew the truth, that his role in my appearance in the world had been marginal and less expansive.

Now, as he took my hand and led me to our apartment building just around the corner on 63rd Road, I searched his pockets for candy. Sometimes, he pretended that he did not know the objective of my hunt and would raise his hands helplessly, the fabric of his wrinkled cotton button-downs riding up against his armpits. I smelled Milky Way, as it had been a few weeks since that candy had entered the rotation, and the sensation of smoky caramel was deeply, knee-shakingly tempting.

"What are you looking for?" Dedushka asked and we stopped right outside of Waldbaum's, customers pushing their way around us to get into the narrow entrance. I noticed that even if it was already May, Dedushka was wearing only his white undershirt beneath his jacket. He took my arm and waited for the signal to cross the street, "Nu, what? Did I forget something at home?" I searched his face for telltale signs of the game—a smile working its way toward the surface of his mouth—but his face was confused, erased of character.

We walked together in silence. When we got to the lobby of my building, I realized that I did not play my favorite game with the tree out in front—"If I can get to it in ten steps, Koshchei will ask me to the dance"—a symptom of a preoccupied mind. Instead, I turned to Dedushka, who was absentmindedly running his fingers through his grizzled stubble, and surprised myself by saying, quickly, breathlessly, "Maybe you can help me. There's this boy, Koshchei the Deathless. He doesn't realize that he and I, we're the same. If he asks me to the dance, I can prove this to him. I think it will change everything."

My grandfather looked down at me and pressed the elevator button. I realized that the pearly white part of his eyes had been invaded by thin, silky threads of red. "I think I understand," he whispered. "I will help you if you will help me." I thought of the missing Milky Way and nodded. The elevator door stirred, rumbled, and with a loud, creaky sigh, slid to a close.

III.

The results of my research on the meaning of Koshchei the Deathless:

My mother (washing dishes): "It comes from Russian fairy tales. Koshchei the Deathless was the most frightening villain. My mother used to threaten me—if you don't eat your beets, Koshchei the Deathless will eat them for you. No, I know that makes no sense, but it was very scary. I don't remember what he looked like, but it was impossible to destroy him. Wait, I think, there was one way—if you found his soul. But it was hidden and you had to trick him to reveal its location. Then he would die."

From *Slavic Myths and Folktales*, an unwieldy coffee table book overdue by a month and a half from the Rego Park Public Library: "The strangest character in Slavic mythology, his spirit lived outside of his body. To discover this alter ego was no easy feat, as it lay inside an egg nestled in the belly of an animal which itself was folded into the body of another animal." A watercolor of Koshchei swam alongside the text. It portrayed a skinny old man on a horse, charging toward the forest, the sword in his gnarled hand extended and curved.

Koshchei (in the ochre-painted halls between English and gym class): "I am the most powerful of Hebrew monarchs. Whatever I decide becomes encoded into human action. I have a legion of supporters, all risking their lives to carry out any command. I cannot be hurt, maimed or annihilated. I am immortal. But if you find my soul, you will sap me of my strength."

Anat Rosenberg (overhearing on the way to the ladies room): "He is beyond a dork. And he smells."

IV.

When we walked into the apartment and shut the door, Dedushka took off his jacket and then put it back on again, realizing he was wearing nothing over his undershirt. His face blazed with shame. Together, we walked into my parents' bedroom and rifled through my father's side of the closet. Identical light-colored shirts hung in a neat row next to dark, scratchy pants. We took out the shirt farthest from the front, a faded yellow button down purchased by my mother at a Flatbush Avenue Odd-Job after we had settled into our first apartment. My father always hated it, insisting it made him look diseased.

I helped Dedushka put the shirt on, one arm at a time, and was surprised to find it loose around the stomach. Was I just too preoccupied with my significant Koshchei concerns to notice this change? When I pictured my grandfather in my mind, I envisioned a vigorous but portly man shrouded in tallis, praying by the cement-colored light of early morning. The man in front of me was sharpened, excesses shaved away.

"Ninochka," he said. "I will help you with this what's-his-name Deathless problem, but you must not tell your parents."

I thought of my former betrayal—did it really matter if I was purchased or created in my mother's belly? The difference between the two suddenly seemed inconsequential. I wanted to explain this to Dedushka, to clear my conscience and erase my growing list of sins against him.

"Tell them what?"

Dedushka sat down on my parents' bed and rocked back and forth, as though in response to a slight push of the hand. Engulfed by my father's shirt, he was flabby skin and muscle, dark spots and hair bristle. "Last month, I forgot your mother's birthday," he said. "I realized this when you brought that plant from school and told me it was a present." His cheeks were moist, something I hadn't seen since the death of my grandmother. "I completely forgot my own daughter's birthday."

I took his hand. "I almost forgot her birthday once, too," I said, though I hadn't, and had a hard time imagining how anyone could—my mother began a voluble search for hidden presents two weeks before her birthday. "It's okay," I said in English.

"That's what I love about America," my grandfather said. "In the end, everything's 'okay.' And maybe that's better." His smile was like a thin, blunt knife.

"I won't say anything," I said, and he nodded. *We understand each other*, his eyes implied.

"Now, let's talk about your dilemma. You say this Koshchei boy doesn't acknowledge you? We will change that. We will find his soul."

V.

For our first assignment, we were told to make a list of all the miracles God created to prove his existence to the desert-traversing Israelites. Having announced this task, Mrs. Gliksberg slumped in her chair and opened up a weathered V. C. Andrews paperback. On the cover, a gaunt blonde girl peeked out of the window of a desolate, bat-infested mansion. On my blank piece of paper, beneath a drawing of an arrow-pierced heart surrounding "N. R. + K," I wrote "bread."

Mrs. Gliksberg turned the page and cast a single wary eye across the room. I recognized the paperback as one that Anat accidentally left behind after morning prayers. Anat had the biggest boobs in our grade, and naturally, the most male attention. Because she had little time to waste on actual schoolwork and was failing almost every class, she understood that to ingratiate herself with Mrs. Gliksberg, she would have to purchase a new V. C. Andrews to find out if the twins ever escaped the attic.

I looked down. In my notebook, I had carefully listed all the potential and confirmed couples for the dance. Koshchei remained alone, a virgin king, but even he would have to cave under the pressure and name his date to the dance.

The whispers coming from his circle were growing louder, forcing Mrs. Gliksberg to put her book down. "Miracles," she growled.

Koshchei looked up at her, a smile playing around his lips. "Yes, I've performed a few of those myself." The Followers tittered, appreciatively. Mrs. Gliksberg narrowed her eyes, making a note in her grade book.

The Ten Commandments, I wrote, unsure if that was a miracle or a natural phenomenon. Just in case, I wrote them all out, in a clean, sloping hand. Did coveting the neighbor's house include Anat's boobs? If so, then I coveted them sometimes—at night, under covers, I searched for hills and crevices while my parents fought in the living room. Head heavy with sleep, hands resting on the tiny nubs of my breasts, I overheard my parents fighting bitterly about medical bills, the astronomical costs of brain scans. But the words never came together in my head and I would fall asleep dreaming of the final dance in Koshchei's arms. Just like in the movies, the whole school would watch us, riveted, as we swayed to Michael Jackson's "Wanna Be Startin' Somethin'."

Out of the corner of my eye, I watched Anat respond to a note, her pencil dotted with images of Marmaduke, her mauve sweater fluffy and tight-fitting. She dropped it behind her with a long manicured finger. She would be the first in the class to turn thirteen—that verdant, mystical age.

Either Mrs. Gliksberg had passed the critical juncture in her novel or she decided she had seen enough of our faces that day, but we were suddenly dismissed. Chairs slid against the floor emitting a sound not unlike chalk scratching the blackboard. I let out a tiny squeal, mimicking the mood of the rest of the kids, and jumped up from my desk, stalled by the uncertainty of where I would go. On the way out the door, I brushed up against Koshchei's elbow.

"I'm sorry."

"Sinner," he said.

"Step away," one peon intoned, holding up his right palm before my nose.

"Do not touch the king, Koshchei," another said, using his Book of Prophets to push me to one side.

Not knowing what to do, I bowed my head as they shuffled out, creating a protective casing around their leader. I wondered what my punishment would be if I penetrated the circle to touch the head of dark curls, my fingers weaving in and out of places where the hair breathed. I imagined I would be stoned, with Mrs. Gliksberg indifferently directing the angle of the rocks while she continued to follow the adventures of the light-haired, incestuous twins. I would probably not struggle, but make precise lists in my head—You Shall Not Give False Testimony Against Your Neighbor—my eyes remaining firmly closed.

VI.

My grandfather and I began to pray together every day after school. Getting off the bus, we walked to synagogue. I climbed the narrow staircase to the nearly empty women's section and took a front row seat, overlooking the tops of heads, some with amoeba-shaped holes in the middle. My grandfather stood rotating in the center, but if I turned my attention elsewhere, he would disappear in the crowd, becoming a grainy, distant body.

I held the Bible in the cradle of my left arm, just like I used to position My Little Pony during her daily feeding. The pages were made of the thinnest paper and the rustling sound they created was the gentlest of whispers. I tried to stifle distracting thoughts and concentrate on a single, beautiful image—an empty playground, the first tentative markings from a newly bought pen, a Little Debbie coffee cake—anything representing the divine. Instead I saw Koshchei, his hand on my shoulder.

"You think this is really helping?" I asked Dedushka one day. I had never experienced this kind of sustained, reverential dialogue with God—at Gan Israel, it had always felt like polite chitchat.

"Of course," Dedushka said. "In fact, one of my prayers for you was that you would be immortal."

"Immortal?"

"Yes, I know if I pray enough this will happen." He saw my wide eyes, slack mouth.

"What about you?"

"Me?" my grandfather said. A car made a right out of nowhere and he held me out of the way, gripping me tightly around my shoulders, almost losing his own balance. "Yes, of course, me too," he said, so quietly I could barely make out the words.

"And what does this have to do with Koshchei?" I asked.

"You will see. After our prayers, only you will be able to find his soul. And once you do that, he will then be forced to ask you to the dance. He has no choice, don't you see?"

I was fascinated with Dedushka's certainty. What he was saying made sense—if immortality was granted to the misunderstood outsider, to the Messiah, like Isaiah promised, then it was obvious that only certain Russian immigrants could live forever. But every evening, I found it harder and harder to say goodnight to Dedushka. I worried about his being alone in his apartment, blocks away, his head falling asleep on the pillow that used to be my grandmother's. Without my careful vigilance, he was vulnerable, exposed to precarious elements. He seemed to feel the same way, because his hugs were tighter and longer, and when we pulled away, his nose was tinged with mauve.

VII.

Preparations for the end-of-the-year dance and the arrival of warm weather were infusing energy into our normally sluggish bodies. Younger boys hung onto their *kipahs* with one hand as they played "It," chasing each other around the schoolyard. Girls drew attention to themselves with skirts that reached the very tops of their kneecaps, with shirts unbuttoned to reveal the slightest pink triangles of flesh. Little snatches of color unobtrusively introduced into the school's decor—a pink balloon there, a rainbow streamer hanging above there.

Notes were being passed in class more feverishly than before, perhaps working out logistics for the evening itself (to meet up at the condiments stand or by the front steps?) or mulling over the best method to reveal to the class that one has formed a new alliance (casually at recess or a more formal announcement in music class?). People generally looked to Anat to solve the more delicate etiquette conundrums; it was understood that she had unfailing instinct and tact.

All the teachers were assigned dance-preparation duties. Mrs. Gliksberg opened Bible class with a call for our favorite Carvel treats. The kids were split evenly between Lollapaloozas and Flying Saucers. It was I who broke the tie with a bid for a Flying Saucer—not a fair contest in my mind, with the Flying Saucer's complex texture of vanilla ice cream and scalloped chocolate biscuit. At this unexpectedly bravura show of decisiveness from an Invisible, eyebrows were raised. For the first time, Koshchei turned around to appraise me.

"A fine choice for a mortal," he said. I sat down, dizzy with praise. My grandfather was right, then. It was beginning to work.

Rabbi Cohen was stuck with the music selection; he rushed through post-prayers morning announcements to wade through donated albums. He seemed overwhelmed by this task, straining to interpret subtext.

Was "What's Love Got to Do With It?" too cynical? Was "Holiday" too hedonistic? What to make of "When Doves Cry"? He probed students and teachers, who shook their heads.

"No one listens to the words," I finally told Rabbi Cohen, having volunteered to work on the music squad. Five of us had to divide the wobbling album tower into the "Yes," "No," and "Maybe" piles. He looked up, Prince album in hand, confused, trying to place me.

"Don't they?" As an older man, he automatically reminded me of my dedushka, except his beard was thick and a rich mocha brown.

"No, they don't," I said. "I'm Nina, by the way."

"Of course you are," he said impatiently, and stood up. I remembered the annual Gan Israel memo to parents: "You have chosen the right place for your beloved children," it said. "Here at Gan Israel every child receives personal attention. We infuse children with love, spiritual understanding and an excellent education they will never forget." I thought of how relieved my parents must have felt every time they received the memo, how its words allowed them a stable heartbeat as they rushed around all day looking for work at hospitals, returning dispirited to the apartment.

I wondered how Koshchei was faring in Decoration. Did he delegate his chores to the Followers or was he sitting patiently in the gym, his slender hand carving images from Exodus out of colored construction paper? I got up to look. A fiery burning bush was tacked to the door, its black tracing lines faint but visible, stopping me from going any farther, as if in warning.

VIII.

My grandfather was not at the bus stop. I waited at the front steps to my building, circling the tree—"He will ask me tomorrow, he will ask me tomorrow, he will ask me tomorrow." I thought about going next door to the newsstand/candy store to beg for a Milky Way on credit, but I imagined my mother's weary limbs splayed out on the bed after sunset, and thought better of it.

Instead, I turned toward 108th Street. Dedushka had been known to spend the morning at Yasha's, reminiscing about the war with the irascible owner who sliced Gouda cheese by the pound. If I had a day off from school, I would sit on a cardboard box filled with a shipment of tinned sardines or Czechoslovakian raspberry jam and listen to them talk. I would ask about the war, what it was like for them to fight the Germans. I had studied the Holocaust in class and was pierced by images of suffering children who looked just like me. Inevitably, Yasha would turn me away with a dollar and say, "If you saw what we saw, you would never sleep again, so go get yourself a treat." I never questioned this imperative.

I strolled past identical high rises and dreary residential homes, my backpack lightly bouncing against my spine. The day was so clear and warm that I could not believe I was experiencing it all alone. The unexpected freedom made my stomach rumble. Or was I dying for a *cheburekh*?

A cheburekh was a hot pastry filled with ground beef and sautéed onions. The best ones were sold from a cart at the mouth of the 108th Street stores by a silent but ornately dressed babushka. I circled around her cart for a while, planning my mode of attack. I finally asked her for a cheburekh, offering my most irresistible smile, promising her that my dedushka was just over at Yasha's and would pay her as soon as he got out. She hesitated, groaned, but reached for one anyway. I relished the first bite, ignoring the tumbling buttery crumbs, and closed my eyes as the fragrant beef began to dissolve in my mouth. The babushka watched me eat, lines of pleasure forming around her eyes.

I continued to Yasha's, passing Russian hardware stores, clothing stores ("European Fashions for Women for Under $10!"), cobblers and purse repairers, Central European psychics, Uzbek restaurants with large chunks of meat corpses rotating in the window. Even on a weekday, the street was a bustling mess of bodies, rushing from store to store as if preparing for the Last Judgment.

But Yasha's International was the hub of all activity. Butcher, grocer, and importer of familiar Russian and Polish canned goods, Yasha's was where all Russians in the entire Rego Park/Forest Hills area finished their journeys. At Yasha's one could unearth the reason Mrs. So-and-so had not been out walking her granddaughter lately or why Mr. So-and-so was no longer strolling 108th Street with his wife or how Ms. So-and-so got ahold of that fur coat, which was absolutely not a fake, this I could promise you.

I pushed my way inside with an oily hand and scanned the store for my grandfather. For a moment, I was distracted by the sight of my favorite dessert, a ball of sweet cheese covered in dark chocolate, a benign cow imprinted on its plastic wrapping. I realized I was still famished but my gut told me that coming here was wrong, that I should have waited at the bus stop, even if I stood there until Waldbaum's closed its doors and turned off all its lights, leaving me alone in the dark. I turned to go, weighing distances and times, dividing the result by a beautiful day and a savory cheburekh.

"Ninochka," I heard, and turned around.

By the section of the glass display case flaunting Stalin sausages, glistening with fat and peppercorns, stood Koshchei's mother, a slight, wispy woman dressed entirely in unflattering brown. Behind her, Koshchei was leaning his forehead against the glass, his hands stuffed in the pockets of his corduroys.

"You know Seryozha, of course," she said, tugging at the sleeve of her son's Members Only jacket.

Yasha called her number, sixty-four, and she walked away, rattling off a long list of deli items in a cool monotone. Koshchei did not change positions, but rolled his forehead back and forth as though it were a pie crust.

"Um, hi . . . Seryozha," I said, discreetly reaching behind me to rub my buttery hands against the fabric of my backpack. My mouth felt oniony and parched. It had been a long time since I'd seen Koshchei without an entourage. He was suddenly reduced to human scale.

"Hi," he said, his voice tinny and unnatural. "So, what are you doing here?"

"Looking for my grandfather," I admitted. "He is not feeling well these days."

"That's too bad," he said, still looking down at sausages, his breath forming phosphorescent steam on the refrigerated display case. "What's wrong with him?"

"I don't know." I didn't want to talk about my grandfather now. Koshchei's mother was coming to the end of her list—salami, something, something, two pounds of cheese, dried apricots.

"So, you going to the dance," I said, my voice flat and mercifully free of nuance.

"Yeah, I guess," he said. His fingers left imprints on the glass. "Wanna go to the dance with me?"

I stopped rubbing my hands and brought them down to my sides. Tomorrow he might say that I petitioned for this position with his secretary or that he drew my name in a royal lottery. He may even create an official-looking document that would carefully outline my responsibilities as his temporary consort. Now he was engulfed in an immaculate baby blue jacket, puckered around his waist and zipped up to the very bottom of his Adam's apple.

"Sure," I said, clenching my jaw, elated.

He looked sideways at me then, as though he was intensely interested in the lower left hand corner of my cheek. He took one hand out of the pocket of his corduroys and popped a Chiclet in his mouth. I waited for his next words, trying not to breathe.

"And don't call me Seryozha," he said. "Ever again." He turned around and swept past his mother out of the store.

I was tempted to stomp my feet against the floor with helpless joy, but I suddenly remembered that I had still not found Dedushka. I needed to tell him that our afternoon prayers at the synagogue had succeeded, that I had discovered the soul of Koshchei the Deathless. It suddenly occurred to me that if Koshchei asked someone else to the seventh-grade dance or grew up or moved, it didn't matter. Even if sometime in the future, he became a famous actor or rock star, or if he simply never spoke to me again, I would always know that his soul lay at Yasha's, on the other side of the refrigerator, wedged somewhere between smoked meats and chocolate-covered cheese.

Running back to the apartment building, I skirted the corner of the *cheburekhi* lady, the wind unsealing the sweater from my perspiring skin. My heart was beating irregularly against my chest as if afraid it may not catch up with the rest of the body, that its contribution to haste just may not be enough.

IX.

The first place I checked was the bus stop to make sure Dedushka was not waiting for me there, hopeful and disoriented. The whole block was quiet and strangely empty, as though a seminal cartoon, like *He-Man*, was on television. I popped into the newsstand, but the gruff Georgian man behind the counter shook his head, no. No Dedushka. Quickly out of options, I headed back to the apartment.

I was greeted with the unexpected sight of my mother opening the door. Her face was drawn, crisscrossed with pain. I bit my lip, prepared to be chastised, but she was silent.

"Where were you, Nina Semyonovna?" she asked quietly, but by the lack of edge in her voice, I understood that her heart did not lay in discipline.

"I went to look for Dedushka," I said, staring at the floor.

She stepped aside to let me pass and I saw Dedushka sitting in his white undershirt on our living room couch. His hands were folded together, as though placed there by an external force. He looked up and smiled, allowing me to kiss his cheek. I gave him a knowing look that I imagined imparted, *When Mama is in the other room, we will discuss, you and I. There is much news.*

"I want to talk to you, Nina," my mother said. "Let's go into the bedroom." I followed her, my backpack still on my shoulders, my mind dissecting and classifying outfit combinations. The new flared pink skirt was certainly a viable option or, alternatively, Old Faithful, the blue silk dress with the giant red bow tie in the front. Everyone always pointed out how the blue highlighted my eye color.

My mother shut the door of the bedroom and sat on the bed. I was instantly reminded of my grandfather on the very same spot, clutching my father's yellow shirt in his hands, his bony shoulder blades rising and falling rapidly. The evening light fell sharply across my mother's face, making her hair look unnaturally, wildly red.

"Dedushka is very ill," she said. "There will have to be some changes. As of tomorrow, you will have to walk home alone from the bus stop." From her pocket, she took out a silver key, smooth and luminous. She looked into my eyes. "Do you understand?"

I nodded, but my mind was numb. I thought of the store where I was supposedly bought. Maybe Dedushka was right all along, like he was about Koshchei, which would make my mother's words meaningless. I looked at her accusingly, sitting small and helpless on a cheap Odd-Job comforter. It was she who could not perceive the existence of miracles.

I took the key and swung open the door to the bedroom. My mother did not follow me and, receding from the room, I heard faint, strangled noises. My grandfather sat on the same spot in the same position.

"Dedushka," I said, instantly recalling the exultation of my recent epiphany. "You were right. We prayed and we found his soul."

I watched my grandfather mentally disperse the film clouding his eyes. He smiled and took my hands in his own. His touch was warm, imparting a tingling sensation of safety.

"Whose soul, Ninochka?" he asked.

"Koshchei the Deathless, of course," I said.

"I'm sorry Ninochka," he shook his head. "I have no idea what you're talking about." For the first time, I noticed that he, my mother, and I shared the same droopy eyelids that lent us a permanent appearance of muted exhaustion.

"Koshchei the Deathless," I said again, as though in incantation. I searched his face but found it authentically blank.

"The fairy tale?" He smiled, shook his head again and seemed to remember something. "But guess what I have."

I said I didn't know. I heard my mother walk into the bathroom and shut the door. The sound of running water seemed to fill up the entire apartment so that I expected us to be lifted and carried away by the force of the stream.

Dedushka stretched out two fists in front of my nose. "Go ahead," he said. "Pick one."

I picked the right fist and unclenched his fingers, one at a time. The first time we played this game was at the airport in Moscow as we stood in the middle of a mob of people weeping and saying goodbye. He saw me standing with trembling knees, clutching my favorite bald doll and bent down before me, his fists outstretched. What lay inside his fists was a promise.

Now, a cherry Jolly Rancher, its wrapper frayed and crumpled, appeared in the center of Dedushka's palm.

"See, don't worry," he said, his eyes awake and twinkling. He helped me unwrap the tart, crimson candy and watched me pop it in my mouth, leaning back on the couch, staring at a distant point over my shoulder. Then, after a very long pause, he smiled. "Yes, Ninochka, everything is going to be okay." I turned around to follow his gaze, praying I would see whatever it was he was seeing.

Neighborhood #3 (Power Out)

Marissa Walsh

I moved to Queens on September 11th, when I walked home with my boyfriend across the 59th Street Bridge (Feelin' Groovy) and never returned to my Brooklyn apartment except to pack it up. On the day of the big blackout, it was no love-in, no Brooklyn Borough President Marty Markowitz greeting us on the Bridge welcoming us home. (I've never even *seen* the Queens Borough President.) On *our* bridge, it was old ladies on the narrow pedestrian walkway, and kids running through the parking lot of traffic trying to get somewhere else. It was discovering the only cool Brooklyn-esque bar/restaurant in the neighborhood, and it burning down a few days later. And the Fish 'n' Chips Shop on the corner becoming a Dunkin' Donuts. Oh, and the coffee shop of my dreams—the one I had been looking for my whole life—being kicked out in favor of luxury condos. One day, as I stood at Queensboro Plaza waiting for the bus, someone threw a cup of coffee from the pedestrian overpass above and it almost landed on my head. Was it some kind of sign? If you try to help the blind lady who lives down the hall cross Queens Boulevard, the Boulevard of Death, she will scream at you at the top of her lungs not to touch her. And the lady next door to her sneaks out in the middle of the night to feed the neighborhood cats (and other things, I'm sure). One time someone in the building stole her cat food, and she left a note reminding the person of the video camera in the lobby. The bag of cat food reappeared. But I once saw her get chased down the sidewalk by the super of the building next door. One time at 3 a.m. a car alarm woke me up, followed by the sound of smashing glass. Some vigilante, 311 having failed him, had taken the matter into his own hands, and while the car's headlights no longer flashed, the alarm did not stop. I thought about calling the cops, but really—perhaps he had done the right thing. But was that car Kitty Genovese? Would *I* have gone outside to help? David Berkowitz lived in Queens. I think of that when I navigate the sidewalks of my neighborhood where people refuse to clean up after their dogs. It's a minefield. You have to walk with your head down. Some people started putting up signs, but it didn't seem to matter.

The Children

Jocelyn Lieu

The dead boy's shrine lay no more than a few paces from my grandmother's kitchen, but if you looked out the kitchen window, you couldn't see it. The window was wide enough, and it framed the right view—the rosaries, flowers, and other mementos left at the fence—but the shrine was obscured by the slats of the Venetian blinds my aunt May always kept tilted half closed. Brown plastic bags, the kind you get from the supermarket, were stuffed into the cracks between the sash and pane. If this wasn't enough, pots of overgrown red chrysanthemums lined the sill. My grandmother loved chrysanthemums. She used to love them for their color and life. After the first stroke, she loved them for the faces of the children she saw in the flowers and leaves.

That afternoon, the three of us, my grandmother, May, and I, sat in the kitchen, not because were eating—we weren't—but because it was the warmest room in the house. May told me they were conserving fuel. Then she said the dead boy's girlfriend wanted to keep candles burning on the spot where he fell, which by an ugly stroke of fate was right outside the chain-link fence that enclosed my grandmother and aunt's narrow side yard.

"Can you imagine?" May said.

I didn't know exactly what she meant, but I nodded. Looking into her eyes, I couldn't help noticing the angry bruises of insomnia underneath. When my grandmother got up each night to wander, May rose, too, long black hair hanging loose around her shoulders, and followed her through a house rife with danger: steep stairs, rings of fire, linoleum worn slick as ice.

May wanted to tell the whole story, and who was I to stop her. The police really did outline the boy's body in chalk, but it rained, then there was that big snowstorm, and by the time the snow melted, the outline was gone. What remained were the beads and crosses, the letters, photographs, and artificial flowers—roses, mostly—whose stems twined like living vines around the steel links. Mourners kept adding to the shrine. May never caught them at it, but each time she left the house, there was something new. A tiny artificial Christmas wreath. A key chain with a miniature basketball attached. Mounds of candle wax glazed the masonry, like stalagmites rising from the floors of caves.

Saying I looked cold, May handed me an afghan, a crocheted splash of clashing colors. She was in the middle of describing how troublesome the dead boy's friends and family had been.

"The mother and the girlfriend actually came to see me," she said. "I told them the shrine was their business, they could keep it as long as they wanted. But not the candles, not with all the trash and leaves flying around. They could go up in flames, then where would we be?"

For some reason, the urgent note in her voice embarrassed me. I nodded, Go on.

"The girlfriend hooked her fingers in the fence. She wouldn't let go. The mother couldn't get her to move. Luckily, a teacher from the high school was there, and he managed to calm her down. 'The ladies are thinking of the fire hazard,' he told her. 'You've got to think of the fire hazard, too.' "

I thought of my grandmother's house, surrounded by pine trees and unpruned hydrangeas, a forgotten patch of forest in the middle of Queens. Before I could push the image away, flames exploded through the branches, licked the windows, feathered the eaves.

"The teacher kept repeating the girl's name, which sounded like Loopy. 'Loopy, Loopy, come on, baby, let's go.' Loopy, Loopy, over and over. As if he was trying to remind her who she was."

My aunt paused. She looked at my grandmother, who was sitting in the straight-backed chair by the refrigerator staring at me, shifting her gaze from me to the chrysanthemums and back again, as she had since I arrived.

"You okay, Ma?" All urgency was gone. Her voice was soft and patient now.

My grandmother wore the angora sweater I had bought her last Christmas. A green penumbra of fuzz radiated from her thin arms.

"The children are happy to see you," she said.

"I don't see any children, Ma," May said gently.

"They don't say much, but they're happy. You know how kids are."

"I don't see any children," May said again.

"They're shy around people they haven't seen in a long, long time. But they'll get used to you."

May glanced at me, to gauge how I was taking this. Although I'd been forewarned, a wave of feeling rushed through me, fast and incomplete, like the ripped-to-shreds dreams you have in the weird sleep of general anesthesia. Ever since she came back from the hospital last summer, my grandmother, who'd slowly faded for years, saw things only she could see. At times her visions were surreal: a woman with flowers that blossomed from her shoulders and neck; another woman trapped inside a box, with her head and arms sticking through. Most often, though, she saw children. They lived under the table and among the chrysanthemums. They whispered, ran, hid in the basement behind the stacks of *National Geographic*s and boxes of roots and herbs from my grandfather's old store. May said the children were black or Chinese, depending, and that my grandmother talked to them and worried over them. She didn't know where they came from, but she understood they'd been abandoned.

Two bobby pins held my grandmother's white-streaked hair away from her face. She looked at me expectantly. I didn't know how to answer, so I smiled. Her eyes moved from side to side, down and up, as if she was trying focus, read me, in English and in Chinese. She seemed dazed, lovestruck, and I found myself longing for the time when her gaze was as clean as a knife.

Turning to May, I said, "What happened? Tell me from the start."

"All right," she said slowly. "I heard the shots. By the time I got to the window, he was already on the ground. At first I thought it was a car backfiring or some kids lighting off M-80s, then people started running over from the high school. I went outside, but didn't go past the gate. A man yelled, 'Call 911, call 911!' so I ran back inside."

"Did my grandmother see?" The moment the words left my mouth, I realized I was using the language of absence, although she was sitting right there.

"You see anything, Grandma?"

Her eyes drifted back to the chrysanthemums. The bottom leaves were dry and brown, but the rust red flowers still smelled pungently fresh.

"No," said May, "I don't think she did."

My grandmother blinked. Understanding seemed to dawn. "Are you hungry? Did you eat?"

"You want a sandwich?" May asked. "There's some turkey and some Swiss cheese. Sorry, but it's all low fat, low salt."

"Low everything," my grandmother said.

Clementines and hazelnut cookies, my offering, lay untouched on two chipped Wedgwood platters. In better days, when my grandmother's eyes were like knives and her black hair was marcelled so smooth it looked like oil or ink, when my grandfather was still alive and my parents and brothers and sisters and I visited every weekend, the same kitchen table was covered with platters of *bao* and sliced red pork, and the *baci*, little kisses, that my grandmother's Chinatown friends brought from Little Italy. Now it was laden with old magazines and bills, her medicines, and the family-size boxes of raisin bran and corn flakes that came from the woman next door. My aunt and the neighbor, who was from Taiwan, swapped commodity cereal for bags of rice. The neighbor received the cereal—which to her was bizarre and inedible—through Aid to Families with Dependent Children. "She doesn't understand corn flakes," my grandmother once explained. "Real Chinese don't drink milk."

"No, thanks," I told May, "I had a late breakfast. Please. I'm fine."

She leafed through the top newspapers on one of the waist-high piles of newspapers near the window, then passed a handful of clippings to me. The *Daily News*, the *Post*, the *Times*. Although I didn't say so, I was surprised the murder had attracted so much attention. In *Newsday*, there was a photograph of the street outside the kitchen window. It took me a moment to understand that the grainy image of an anonymous brick house surrounded by an anonymous chain-link fence was, in fact, my grandmother's. More than the shrine outside the window, the sting of recognition made the crime seem real.

Among the uniformed officers were two plainclothesmen in raincoats, one of whom held a Styrofoam cup with steam rising from its mouth. Crime-scene tape stretched from the fence post to the stop sign on the corner. I could actually make out the words, SCENE DO NOT CROSS CRIME SCENE DO NOT.

Beneath that photo was a studio portrait of a kid with close-cropped hair. He was black—no, Latino. Jason P. Veracruz. Jason P. Veracruz wore a tuxedo. He looked younger than sixteen, the number that followed his name. Scanning the first few paragraphs, I discovered that he was a popular student, a member of the debate team. On the afternoon he died, he left school to buy an orange soda and a bag of potato chips, and was on his way back when he was shot twice in the abdomen and once in the neck, the fatal wound. According to the police, he was killed because he refused to give up his gold chain.

The reason for the media attention was now clear. The story of Jason Veracruz's death was a chapter in a book of stories so similar they could all be the same: a nice kid, a senseless death over a chain, a jacket, a pair of athletic shoes. The moral of the story had something to do with devalued lives and the times, and how terrible the city was, but sitting in my grandmother's cold kitchen that winter afternoon, I couldn't think of morals. Everything fell apart.

"I talked to the reporters, but first I made them swear not to use my name," May said. "I talked to the cops, too. I guess that makes me a witness, even if I told them over and over I didn't see anything."

The last light angling through the blinds striped the dusty chrysanthemums. I wondered what May *did* see. How had she occupied herself all those hours while police and reporters milled outside the house measuring, drinking coffee, taking pictures, making notes, taping their words of warning across the fence?

That winter, May was forty-nine. The youngest daughter, she never left home. For ages, it seemed, she tended to my ailing grandfather, traveling with him over the long, slow arc that led to his death a dozen years ago. May was forty-nine, but with her black hair and smooth skin, she could have been my sister. She was wearing jeans, a sweatshirt, and Frye boots, her usual uniform. In the days when they still had visitors, someone, somebody white, asked why she always wore boots, and she said, "Because my feet are bound."

She rarely went out, only to shop at Key Food or to take my grandmother to the doctor. I have to admit that her behavior didn't seem that strange—except in those rare, awful moments when I stopped to think about the situation. Then my grandmother and aunt changed shape before the eye of memory. They swelled, grew distorted, became the women you heard about in another, older volume of stories: the shut-ins, recluses, the witches nobody sees. The hand that lifts the curtain and lets it fall back into place.

"The children are frightened," my grandmother was saying.

"Frightened?"

"People yell at them and hit them for no reason. You can't blame them for being scared."

With a guilty start, I realized she'd been listening all along.

"They have suspects," May said, "but I'm not going to testify, not in a million years. Those guys have to be crazy, shooting that kid like that, in broad daylight. They're crazy, and crazy people can do anything. Like burn down a house."

"They won't burn the house down."

"How do you know?"

"They won't."

"You don't think." It wasn't a question. May looked toward the window, and I followed her eyes. "That fucking shrine," she said.

My breath stopped, but my grandmother was staring off into space. "The shrine's like an arrow pointing at us, saying it happened here, *this* is the place."

Her voice had grown almost loud, louder than I'd ever heard it before. "It says *this, this, this! This* is the house where somebody died."

My heart was beating so hard I could feel the pulse in my throat. If she said another word, we would implode, wrapped in flames.

May stared at her hands, which gripped her knees. I groped for the right comforting words, anything to keep her from talking, from declaring what had been welling up inside her for years.

"Don't worry, they'll forget," I said. "When the shrine comes down, they'll forget. People have short memories these days."

Silence told me I'd said the wrong thing. May glared, then turned away. After a moment she began to pack my hazelnut cookies back into their box. Before I knew it, she had wrapped and retied the box with the red string from the bakery.

"Take them with you," she murmured, her voice shrunk back to normal. "We don't eat this kind of stuff anymore. Take them, so they won't go to waste."

She was smiling, but I kept seeing the glare she gave me the moment before, the bitter eyes that said, *How do you know? How do you know anything?*

A half hour later, my grandmother leaned toward May and said something in Cantonese. May nodded, then told me I should go before it got too dark. Relieved and sad, I folded the afghan and placed it on top of the newspapers. When I kissed my grandmother's cheek, I breathed in her dry old woman's smell, the acrid scent of chrysanthemums.

The time came to kiss my aunt. Her face softened a little. "Take care of yourself, kiddo."

"I'll be back soon."

"It's good to see you," my grandmother said. "It's always good." She tried to tuck something into my hand, a folded bill, a five. She must have been holding it all along, through the hours I sat with them both.

"No, Grandma, don't."

"Take it. Just take it," said May.

Before I fully understood how I got there, I was out past the pine trees, the hydrangeas. The air was sharp and cold. Twenty-five years ago, when my brothers and sisters and I were children, we helped May bury steel wool around the roots, to bring color to the flowers. I never knew if we were responsible for the pale blue, or if it was just an idea we had. May's hair gleamed in schoolgirl braids, and now I remembered the odor of damp earth, the cold, gritty feel of it under my nails.

It was starting to snow. I swung the gate open. When I looked back at the kitchen window, the light was on. My grandmother and May peered through the Venetian blinds. All I saw were two dark forms, one taller than the other. I waved, wondering what they could see. Someone had set out three new votive candles and lighted them. The flames roared softly in the wind.

Flight

Rigoberto González

When hair sticks to the floor this way, resisting the bristles of the broom, it means that the client's sweating heavily, that the barbershop's too hot, but the man growing warm beneath the nylon cape is too much man to complain. The beads of perspiration swell on his face and drop—signs of suffering—but he keeps silent, surrendered to the barber who *has* to notice and hand him a towel eventually, maybe even suggest what he will not: *turn on the fan, open the window.* Tavi stops and rests both hands on the tip of the broomstick, his chin on top of his hands to resist the urge to wipe the client's forehead without being asked. He keeps his distance and must never do what he's not told to do. It will keep Donato from swatting him on the side of the head.

"Open the window, Tavi," Donato calls out as he shapes the fade, though at first Tavi hears, "Don't be a pussy, Tavi," but he corrects himself when he notices the client's shoulders react: relief is near.

Tavi opens the window because the fan isn't working. The shears, the clippers, the lathering machine will be all the music this afternoon. The boom box isn't working either. The television hasn't worked in years and stares blankly from the corner of the room. It's the shop's only useless mirror, though Tavi can see the bright window's miniature version on the screen, his stick-thin body bending down to let the airplanes in.

"Let the airplanes in," his father says at home, meaning, "Open the window." Both at home and at work, opening the window lets in the same noise. Home is less than a block away. LaGuardia not far from the neighborhood. Elmhurst right under the path airplanes take to the landing strip. Each airplane like the groan of an angry god.

183

Tavi wants to wait and greet the next one, but then Donato says, "How's that?" And the client answers, "That's fine. Thanks, man." Another buzz cut completed, another wipe across the chair damp with sweat. *"Tavi!"* Donato says, pointing to the glistening seat. *Tavi,* the sound of his name like cracking a wet towel in the air.

Tavi rushes over, reaching for the rag stuffed into his back pocket. From the corner of his eye, he catches the brief exchange of money, the handshake, the client posing in front of the mirror one last time before he heads outside to charm the world.

"Come-mierda," Donato says when he pockets the money. It means the tip is low.

Donato yanks the boom box cord out of the socket and wraps it around his hand like a bandage. "I'm going to get this piece of crap looked at," he says.

"What about the fan?" Tavi says, and then immediately regrets it.

Donato glares at him. *"Qué vaina,* just keep the window open," he says. "I'll be right back. If a client comes, sit him down on the goddamn chair. *Coño."*

Donato walks off with the boom box beneath one arm, the other reaches for the cigarettes. Tavi sticks his head out the window and watches him turn the corner. On hot summer days like this no one's out on the streets and men are least likely to come in for a cut.

Across the way, the old Haitian woman with a wrap around her head props a pillow on the sill and leans on it. She's keeping watch over the street as well. For one brief moment she makes eye contact with Tavi but quickly moves on. She has seen him as many times as he's seen her. Nothing new here. She knows all of his shirts. He knows all of her wraps.

Tavi wishes his father could stare out the window at home. The reason Tavi lets the airplanes in is because his father can't come out. The wheelchair's too heavy for him to maneuver. Or rather, he doesn't even try to roll himself a single inch, so he sits in the kitchen with enough food on the table to get him through the day, until Tavi comes home to carry him to the toilet. It's like taking care of a cat that will look after itself for extended periods of time. The small television on the counter keeps him entertained, though usually his father just dozes off. In case of an emergency, the phone's within reach; the shop's number on speed dial. If it weren't for the back pain, he'd rather stay in bed.

If it weren't for the stroke, Tavi's father might still be cutting hair at his old shop instead of sending Tavi over just to get him out of sight. But Tavi takes his job seriously anyway. It's the only place he ever gets to go. Lately even those trips seem numbered. His father used to say that a barbershop will never fold because no matter what the trends on the street there's always someone in need of a cut and with enough cash in his pocket to pay for it.

"The *mama-huevo* economy," Donato says, explaining why each month his clientele goes down. It's better than admitting that all the young men prefer to head to Flava Cutz, which has eight barber stations, loud Daddy Yankee and Pitbull, and a mirror that covers the entire south wall, the reflection of the entire shop doubled because it's cool.

"Just check it out quickly and report," Donato ordered Tavi when he first heard of the new barbershop.

Tavi's knees began to shake. "To Queens Boulevard?" The large yellow warning signs A PEDESTRIAN WAS KILLED CROSSING HERE flashed through his mind.

"Nothing's going to happen to you," Donato said. "*Coño*, I'd go if it didn't look like I was just sizing up the competition. It's less suspicious to have *you* stumble in. Just act natural."

Donato was wrong. Tavi along Queens Boulevard was the most unnatural act. It was like jumping into the current of the river without knowing how to swim, so he held his breath as long as he could, his eyes wide open and his cheeks inflated. And in order to avoid crossing all those lanes, since the shop was on the south side of the boulevard, he used the subway underpath, where the stench of urine made him think his father was nearby, ready to yell at him for daring to go beyond the block.

"What the fuck's wrong with *him?*" he heard someone say.

When he got to the shop, Tavi saw a world he had been denied: youth. The laughter and palm slapping of the young, the way their shoulders swayed when they walked across the room, the way their skins glowed with cologne and perspiration at their aggressive displays of male affection—all of it was a theater he had only seen from afar all these years. He stood staring from the sidewalk for nearly thirty minutes and not once did one of them notice him. He remained invisible, as he had always been.

"Well?" Donato asked when Tavi returned to the shop. Tavi had retraced his steps back, except that he had come back wiser about the ways of the beautiful world—the world he didn't occupy.

"It's beautiful," Tavi reported, and Donato swatted him on the side of the head. But that night, and for many nights afterward, Tavi lay in bed fantasizing about walking into Flava Cutz and asking them if they needed a janitor to sweep the floor or wipe the mirrors or seek out more neck strips—anything to be within the arm's length of their body heat, to be close to the men who were virile and young and to be reckoned with.

Suddenly, the shop door opens and a man walks in. "Are you open?" he asks.

Tavi's shaken out of his daydream, but he's too stunned to speak. "Okay," the man says to himself. "Are you alright, buddy?"

Men are not supposed to be this beautiful. Or rather, beautiful men don't come into Donato's shop. They go to Flava Cutz. Here, they get old men with weak dentures, who have been coming in for so many years, they still remember the previous barber, Tavi's father, and will ask about him. And sometimes the random man in his forties, like the one who was just here, walks in on impulse. But not men like this with perfect lips and perfect skin, the cheekbones and eyebrows perfectly primped and even. Tavi runs his tongue along his crooked set of teeth.

"Donato will be right back," Tavi says, shaken out of his spell.

The perfect man nods his head.

"You can take a seat," he says, motioning to the barber's chair.

The man nods his head again and sits down. He considers himself in the mirror, raises one hand and runs the tips of his fingers along the arc of his upper ear. On his wrist, a bracelet with tiny representations of the religious figures Tavi's mother left behind when she died—*Santo Niño de Atocha, Ángel de la Guarda, Virgen de Guadalupe.* The man notices Tavi staring. He turns around. "Octavio," he says, holding out his hand, the bracelet.

"Yes," Tavi says, extending his own hand. "But everybody calls me Tavi." He's embarrassed suddenly that he's still carrying around the nickname the old men gave him when Tavi was the unfortunate son of the barber who lost his wife when his son was only five years old.

"That's funny," the man says. "I meant, my name's Octavio. But I guess yours is, too. What a coincidence, right?"

Tavi freezes again. Octavio and Octavio, like the matching pairs on a domino tile. Tavi, with the scent of tonic and disinfectant; Octavio with the scent of cologne as strong as solid wood, his skin taut and pulsing with the pores of a man who goes to the gym.

"When's your birthday?" Tavi asks.

"Say what?" Octavio says. He lets out an uncertain laugh, but then adds, "July 12."

"Mine's on July 21," Tavi says. His eyes widen.

"And what does that mean, that we're like soul mates or something? Crazy."

Before Tavi can explain what it means, Donato comes back, excited to have a client waiting on the chair. He comes up to shake Octavio's hand and swats Tavi away. "Give the man some breathing room, will you, Tavi? Sorry about that, *muchacho.*"

"Nah, it's cool," Octavio says. "We were just shooting the shit. It turns out we have the same name, and that we're born in the same month. I think we're twins separated at birth or something." Both men burst out laughing. Tavi reddens. But then Donato says, "Tavi, go dig out some more razor blades, will you? I'm running low." The business at hand continues.

Some clients shut their eyes during a cut, others keep a close eye on the barber's job, and still others let their eyes lock on any movement they can catch through the mirror, except those who come in wearing glasses. Those men are usually near-sighted and stare helplessly into space. Octavio is the eyes-shut type, though he keeps a conversation going with Donato the entire time.

"So do you think that spic De la Hoya's really going to hang up the boxing gloves for good, or is he bullshitting again?"

"Who knows? Well, he can always go back to that singing career he put on hold."

"*Coño*, I hope not!" Donato says, and they laugh.

Tavi suspects Octavio keeps his eyes shut because he's getting looked at. The shape of his head is perfect. His hairline is perfect, the backs of his ears—beautiful, symmetrical ears, not alien-looking appendages like on most men—perfect. Every once in a while Octavio opens his eyes and notices Tavi. This excites Tavi, getting noticed by the perfect man.

"Tavi!" Donato says, waving him over. The towel-cracking sound again. And then an airplane coming in stops Tavi in his tracks and he rushes back to the window. The magic of the engine cuts through the sky loud and long. It will not be ignored.

"He's never been on one. Can you believe it?" Donato tells Octavio. "Thirty-five years old and never been on one."

Octavio doesn't respond, though he probably understands the code. Donato's telling him that Tavi isn't like normal men. Even if Octavio has never been on a plane either, it's not the same as Tavi never being on a plane. Perhaps Octavio never goes anywhere by choice, but Tavi, he never will.

"Tavi, go get me some water from Chong's, will you?" Donato says. Tavi is devastated that he has to leave on an errand. To Chong's of all places, where business is slower than this one, where no one hurries in or out.

Reluctantly, Tavi takes the five-dollar bill from Donato and walks out into the heat, away from Octavio. He glances back one last time and sees the perfect man sitting there, becoming more perfect still each time the razor caresses the surface of his perfect scalp.

Out on the sidewalk he considers walking faster, but the heat's holding him back. The old Haitian woman looking out the window follows him with her eyes all the way to the corner. *Chong's.*

When he was younger, Chong worked the register himself, but then he grew old, and then he died, and then the bodega was sold to the Koreans, but everyone still calls it Chong's. The Koreans don't care. They didn't even bother to change the name on the sign over the awning.

"Go get me a pack of cigarettes from Chong's," his father used to say. "Go get a beer for Emilio." And Chong would hand over the cigarettes and beer to little Tavi without any money changing hands. Tavi's father would take care of the debt eventually.

That was a different time, when kids could be entrusted with chores like those. When a man like Emilio could sit on the extra chair all day and everyone knew he wasn't waiting in line for a cut. If he ever needed a cut, Tavi's father simply walked over and clipped the sideburns, which were the only parts that grew anymore. Now Emilio was dead and so was Chong. And his father slumped on his wheelchair all day, waiting for his turn to die.

Tavi walks in and out of the bodega, heads back to the shop, but by the time he steps inside, Octavio's gone. Tavi stands there with his armpits damp, a row of salty beads over his lip, which he sucks into his mouth. The crumpled cape over the chair looks like a cocoon that has just released its butterfly. Tavi has the urge to hold it, smell the ghost of the perfection that has walked away.

"Here's your water," Tavi says, begrudgingly.

Donato takes the water with one hand. With the other, he slaps Tavi across the face.

It takes a minute for Tavi to orient himself again.

"What are you, a *pato?*" Donato says.

For a second this confuses Tavi. He hasn't heard the word in a while. Puerto Ricans say *pato.* They mean *maricón,* what his father would say because he's Mexican. "*Maricón! Puto, mama-huevo!*" every time Tavi had to bathe him.

Pato: quack-quack. Fag, queen, *reina,* the kids say.

"Why did you keep staring at that guy? You were making him nervous. He'll never come around here no more," Donato says. "That's another one lost to Flava Cutz."

The severity of the statement sinks in. Octavio will never come back. Tavi has lost his perfect double. It stings more than the slap across the face.

"Go home and check in on your father," Donato commands. "You're making my stomach turn."

Tavi wobbles out of the shop and heads left. The old Haitian woman across the way is also gone. The window gapes out onto the street like a toothless mouth.

When he enters the house, Tavi expects to see his father asleep, but he's wide awake for a change.

"What did you do this time?" his father says without turning away from the television screen.

Tavi doesn't need to answer. It doesn't matter. It's just another day he has disappointed his father.

"All this shit on the news," his father says. "Makes me want to roll the chair to the middle of the street and be done with it."

Tavi turns off the television, clears the table and without having to ask he guides his father's chair to the bathroom, where he will help him onto the toilet and wipe him clean after he's done. When Tavi gets closer to his father, the odor of urine and rancid breath assaults his nose, kills the last traces of Octavio's scent.

Tavi's father wants scrambled eggs for dinner. He's limited to soft foods now that most of his teeth are gone. When he still had a full set and the paralysis was new, Tavi's father bemoaned the fact that he never taught Tavi how to cook, that he spent most of the evenings swatting his son out of the kitchen. For many years afterward, Tavi taught himself through trial and error. Mostly error, which his father threw off his plate for Tavi to clean.

"Put more mayonnaise on it," his father says as soon as Tavi places the plate in front of him.

"Cholesterol, Papa," Tavi says.

His father reaches down to the plate, and then splatters a handful of scrambled egg at Tavi. He started doing this when he could no longer spit.

Tavi lets the egg run down his shirt as he sits to eat.

"Anything exciting down at the shop?" his father asks, taking a spoonful of egg.

"The boom box broke," Tavi offers.

"Goddamn Donato," his father says. "He pushes the buttons too hard."

They eat in silence after that. His father chews with his mouth open and licks his lips clean when he's done. He then belches, farts, and belches again before slumping down on his seat like a deflated balloon.

"I wonder if Emilio's coming over to play dominoes," his father says. "Goddamn Donato, the boom box." He's sleepy. He becomes disoriented when he's sleepy. So Tavi rolls him over to the bedroom.

His father's body feels weightless now. Or maybe Tavi has done this so many times that it's like breathing, no effort at all. He lifts him up to the bed, stretches his legs out and pulls off his sweatpants. The underwear is slightly soiled, but Tavi will wait until tomorrow to change him, just in case he wets the bed.

Tavi expects his father will play dominoes in his dreams, resurrecting his old playing buddies—Emilio, Rorro, Santi and sometimes Chong, who used to live a few doors down. All of them reaching into the center of the table to mix the tiles, the sound of bone striking bone. The sound of bone scratching wood as they claimed their playing pieces. And then the faces pairing up, the domino snake coming together, inch by inch. But now the domino box sits neglected like a closed coffin, buried in a drawer somewhere, because Tavi's father is the only player left.

Back in the day they stayed up until midnight or until someone's wife sent a death threat of "get back home or else" to one of the players, whichever came last. They all had sons but none was interested in coming over to play with Tavi. They all had daughters and all of them were afraid of him. *Loco Tavi, Looney Tavi, Lelo Tavi.* So he sat around mostly, just watching the game, startled whenever one of the men slapped a tile onto the surface too hard.

Once in a while, one of the men would take pity on him and hand him a dollar, tell him to go buy himself a candy bar. But as soon as Tavi grew too old for candy bars the old men ignored him, except when they needed him to fetch a beer from the fridge.

Since Tavi can remember, his life has been constrained to this block. Even the school, where he flunked three times and was able to drop out as a sixteen-year-old eighth grader, was less than a block away. The only time he ever moved beyond the block was when his father had the stroke, and Tavi had to sit in the hospital waiting room until his buddies arrived.

That night was also the only time he didn't sleep at home. He slept at Emilio's house, in his son's room. Donato was kind then, embracing him in the dark while Tavi cried for his father. And then, years later, when Donato took over the shop, Donato stopped loving him. A decade of lovelessness.

Tavi pulls the covers over his father and backs out of the room, closing the door. He goes all over the house and closes every window. It's time to keep the airplanes out. What a surprise then, when he gets to the south window facing the back street that the young people own when the day ends. It's Octavio standing under the streetlight with two kids in front of him.

When Octavio suddenly looks back, Tavi blushes but doesn't hide. Octavio motions to his cohorts, who turn around and snicker.

"Hey, Tavi!" the black kid says. "Come here!"

Tavi's body spasms. In all these years of watching the young men congregate he has never been invited over. He has been teased, whistled at, and a few times they threw rocks or empty beer bottles in his direction, but never this.

The other kid, Santi's grandson, waves. "Come *here!*" he commands. More snickering. Octavio smiles his perfect smile, his teeth sparkle like shiny domino tiles.

Tavi looks over at his father's bedroom. The door is shut. The old paralytic is out and won't wake up, even if he pisses on himself. Suddenly his heart starts to beat faster. He'll go outside and join the guys.

Something new courses through his body, as if he's pumping different blood. It pushes him out the front door that much quicker, and before he realizes it, he's standing a few feet away from Octavio and the two kids.

Octavio nods. Tavi recognizes this nod. It is friendly, it is beautiful. He gets closer.

"Hey, Tavi," Octavio says. "I didn't get to say good-bye earlier."

"Good-bye," Tavi says, and the kids laugh, Santi's grandson covering his mouth with his hand, which has a flower tattooed at the base of the thumb.

"Yeah," Octavio says. "Anyway, I was talking to Darryl and Manny here, and we were thinking about going on a little trip."

"To Brooklyn?" Tavi says. The kids mock him, but Octavio protects Tavi, shushes them.

"Actually, to the islands," Octavio says. "Ever been to the islands? To the D.R.?"

Tavi shakes his head. His father only longed for Mexico, a country he left long before Tavi was born, and which he never returned to.

"You want to come along?" Octavio says. "We're *flying* there."

Tavi's struck numb by the magnitude of the moment. Not only might he leave the block, he might even leave the country. By plane. But it's the possibility of keeping Octavio's company that overwhelms him the most. This is too much for him. He feels as if he's just gotten slapped across the face again. He stumbles a little and this only incites more laughter.

"I have to go home now," Tavi says.

"Okay," Octavio says. "But think about it. It's a weekend trip. Meet us here tomorrow by six if you want to come along."

Octavio stretches his hand out and Tavi takes it, zeroes in on the bracelet. It's the perfect wrist on the perfect man. Tavi walks back to the house, euphoric. Not even the cackling of Darryl and Manny can bring him down.

When he gets home he immediately runs to the back window. Octavio's still there with the two kids. It's not his imagination, it's real. The invitation's real. Even when they don't turn around to look at him the rest of the time they stand under the streetlight, he believes it happened.

When Octavio and the kids walk away eventually, Tavi feels the pang of abandonment, so he lies down on his bed and presses his fists to his chest. He surrenders to the merciful watch of his mother's saints—their portraits slowly going dark on the wall. This is how he coped during recess all those years, when no one would ask him to play, when he wanted to play but was denied entry into the circle of friends. The only time he stood at the center was when those circles of laughter were circles of ridicule: *Loco Tavi, Looney Tavi, Lelo Tavi.*

Tavi rolls over on his fists, giving his back to the memory hovering above him. The saints are now around Octavio's wrist. Octavio will protect him. Octavio will stop the teasing. Octavio will bring out the Octavio in Tavi. A familiar stirring in his pants makes him grind his hips into the mattress. He hasn't felt this sexually excited since his trip to Flava Cutz. But he's not a *pato*; he's not a *reina*. He just wants to belong and be loved.

Tavi still feels high the next morning as he dresses his father and props him up on the wheelchair. He hums while cooking breakfast.

"What the hell happened to you last night," his father says. "Did you finally get laid?"

"Actually," Tavi says. "I got invited to the D.R."

His father laughs. "You? You don't even know where the fuck that is. Or *what* the fuck that is. Who invited you?"

Tavi shakes his head proudly. "A friend."

"*You* have a friend?" his father says. "I see. What's his name, Rockefeller? Rockefeller's taking you to the D.R. on his private jet? Is that it?"

"Say what you will, Papa, I'm going."

His father's mouth drops. "What the—you're completely out of your mind. I know you're stupid but you can't be *this* stupid. How the hell do you think that's possible? You've never even been on a plane before. You'll have a heart attack before it even takes off. Do you realize how terrible it is to ride an airplane?"

Tavi stops in his tracks. He hadn't considered that point. "What does it feel like?" he asks.

"It's like getting shot out of a cannon," Tavi's father says. "And you better pray that the plane doesn't splatter you all over the runway when it lands."

A chill runs through Tavi's veins, but he refuses to let his fear show. "Do-do-do you want some more eggs for breakfast, Pa-pa-pa?" he says in a dry voice.

"No," Tavi's father says. "I don't want you to be late to the shop. You go on and yank this nonsense out of your head. Never stray beyond the block. You'll get hurt."

Tavi shakes nervously the rest of the morning: at home, while he's setting his father's lunch and adjusting the television; at work, while he's cleaning combs and shaking the neck dusters.

"What's the matter with you?" Donato says. "Open the window, will you? Before it starts to get hot in here again."

But Tavi doesn't want to let the airplanes in. So he hesitates.

"Open the goddamn window, *coño!*"

When Tavi opens the window, the noise of a plane flying overhead floods into the room, knocking him down.

"*Carajo*, what has gotten into you this morning? Someone give you drugs?" Donato nudges Tavi up with his foot. "Get up before someone comes in and sees you lying there like a *tecato*."

Tavi stands up and stares down at his feet.

"What's the matter with you, huh?"

Tavi rubs his eyes. The gesture softens Donato a bit, so he asks again, lowering his voice this time: "What's going on, Tavi? Someone's been mean to you?"

Tavi shakes his head. Donato comes closer and places his arm around Tavi's shoulder. Tavi's heartbeat quickens. It's just like the night of his father's stroke, when Tavi had to share a bed with Donato. Their intimacy began this way: first a comforting arm around the shoulder, then a caress along the jaw, then a kiss. Tavi shakes Donato off his body.

Donato's startled by the gesture. His voice strengthens. "Then what? Come on, let's have it. I don't have all day."

"What does it feel like to fly?"

Donato furrows his brow, and then just as quickly he stretches it open in amusement. "Now who would be cruel enough to put something like that in your head?" he says. "No use worrying about something that's never going to happen, Tavi. No use worrying about it." Donato shakes the capes off and begins to fold them.

"Does it feel like getting shot out of a cannon?" Tavi persists.

Donato rolls his eyes. "Alright, if I tell you will you promise not to bother me the rest of the day?"

Tavi nods.

Donato sighs. "Well," he says. "It tickles the stomach a little bit, especially the first time around. But it's just like riding in the backseat of a car going fast."

"Like on a bus?" Tavi says.

"Faster," Donato says. "Like maybe an ambulance. It's bulky but it gets somewhere fast. And it's safe because nothing gets in the way."

"And how about when it lands?" Tavi asks.

"Just like coming to a red light with plenty of warning. No surprises there either. There. Are you happy?"

Tavi nods.

"Good, now get to putting all these things away, I'm going to get a cup of coffee."

For the rest of the day Tavi's satisfied with Donato's answers. But a strange sensation still gnaws at him about why his father would want to keep him from going on a trip. And then it dawns on him: because Tavi takes care of him. If Tavi leaves, who will take his father to the bathroom? Who will make his eggs in the morning?

The day goes by quickly for a change. Tavi keeps to himself, which pleases Donato, and all the while as he sweeps hair and wipes off razors, Tavi comes up with the perfect plan to fly away to the D.R. with Octavio, the perfect man. The plan is this: to leave someone in charge of Papa for the weekend. He's got it all figured out.

When five o'clock rolls around, Tavi doesn't even bother saying anything as he walks out of the shop before closing time, and neither does Donato ask for an explanation.

"You're home early again?" his father says as soon as Tavi comes in. "Don't let me find out you're getting in Donato's way. If he kicks you out don't think I'm going to have you sit around here all day watching television."

Tavi rolls his eyes.

"Don't you roll your eyes at me, *maricón*. I'm still your father."

Tavi grabs his father's wheelchair and jerks it away from the table.

"What the—"

"You're going on a little trip too, Papa," Tavi says.

"A trip? Where? Where are you taking me? Let go of me," his father says, flinging his arms back. Tavi dodges the swollen knuckles.

When they get to the bed, Tavi's father tries to resist even more. "It's too early for bed!" he protests. But Tavi doesn't put his father to bed. He brings his father's body down on the floor.

"You're crazy! Someone! Help!"

Tavi bends down and covers his father's mouth. "Quiet, old man," he says. "Look. You let me go on this trip or I will never come back and then who's going to wipe your ass?"

The threat calms his father down.

"Where are you going? What are you going to do with me?"

"I told you, I'm going to the D.R. for the weekend. And *you're* going to the hospital."

"The hospital? No, they're mean to me there. They won't take good care of me."

"Just for the weekend, Papa," Tavi says. "I promise."

"Please! Please!" Tavi's father begs, letting go of tears this time.

"Stop it!" Tavi says. "You owe me, Papa. You owe me good, and you know it. Don't think I don't know about the money you get from the government."

"And how else are we supposed to eat," his father stammers. "Your mother abandoned us, you know. She was a drunk. She even drank when you were still inside of her, which is why you were born a retard."

"I'm not a retard, Papa," Tavi says. "I'm slow because you never let me go anywhere."

"There's nowhere to go," his father says. "Where do you want to go?"

"To the D.R."

"Don't be an idiot! Pick me up!" His father bangs his fists against the floor. "Can't you see someone's playing a joke on you?"

"No one's playing a joke on me!" Tavi says. "Shut up!" Tavi raises his hand and his father covers his head in protection.

"Now you just lie there," Tavi says. "It's my turn to enjoy some time with my friends. So you better keep your mouth shut for a change. You better not tell the ambulance people that I put you on the floor. Tell them that you fell, that I'm out of town. I'll come to the hospital and pick you up when I return. Will you do that for me, Papa, just this time, pretty please?"

After a brief silence, Tavi's father closes his eyes and nods in resignation. Tavi leaves him there, the door propped open so that the paramedics can see him right away as they come in. He then goes to his room and packs a few items—an extra pair of shorts, a shirt and socks. His toothbrush. He blows kisses at the saints. And then he goes over to the cupboard beneath the sink and pulls out his father's cash box. He spills every last coin into the backpack. If this is going to be the only time, it might as well be a good time. He already sees himself in the D.R., wherever that is, standing underneath the streetlight that pours over Octavio like a rain of gold. And Tavi will be the envy of all the other kids who happen to be looking out their back windows.

Next, the call. He clears his throat, picks up the phone and dials 9-1-1. "Hello," he says in the raspiest voice he can muster. "I've fallen off the bed. *Necesito ayuda, por favor.*"

The dispatcher asks him to confirm the home address. Yes, that's correct.

"And please hurry," Tavi pleads.

His father keeps his head toward the open bedroom door and simply watches wide-eyed as Tavi runs back and forth.

"The ambulance will be here soon," Tavi says. "Remember: play sick."

Tavi looks at the clock. It's still early. He steps out of the house and is about to run to the back street to meet up with Octavio, when suddenly a pang of guilt stops him. Perhaps he should wait for the ambulance to show up, to make sure he sees the paramedics take his father away to safety. He scurries over to the side of the house. By the time he presses his body against the wall, the ambulance sirens announce its arrival.

Unlike what he's seen on television, there doesn't seem to be much of a rush here. The paramedics take their time walking up the steps and walking in. Minutes later, Tavi's heart stops when he actually sees the gurney get rolled out of the house, his father strapped tightly to the metal frame, an oxygen mask over his mouth. His father looks more frail among the able bodies that surround him. Tavi thinks his father spots him as he's hoisted up into the ambulance, so he jerks his body back. No, he couldn't have seen him, not that far away. The lifting of his hand, the twitching of his fingers, just so, could have meant he was waving good-bye to the house, not to his son, who was standing just out of reach.

Tavi looks around for signs of Octavio and nothing. It's already six o'clock. Two minutes pass, then another two. That's when he spots Manny, Santi's grandson, walking out of his house. This is it, he thinks, but then Manny starts to bounce a basketball on the sidewalk. And then his cell phone rings and he sits on the steps, both feet rolling the ball as if he's got nowhere else to be.

Tavi attempts to wave at him, to let him know that he's waiting, that he's made it, but Manny doesn't see him. Tavi's afraid to yell because the ambulance is still parked in front. And then Manny goes back into the house, leaving the ball to roll on its own for a few seconds before it stops cold at the fence. It simply sits there and will likely stay there all evening, without direction. Empty house, empty street, and Tavi feels like the lonely black line on *la cajita*, the domino with the two expansive blanks. Another minute passes, then another. "You want to come along? We're *flying* there," Octavio promised.

Suddenly everything speeds up: the closing of the ambulance doors, the paramedics climbing back into the cabin, the driving away. And that's when Tavi hears it: an airplane flying above him, a harsh, invasive noise that collapses the entire sky on top of him. That's *his* airplane. He missed it. Octavio has gone off to the D.R. by himself. And now his father, too, is flying off without him.

And then the world splits in two. On one side, Octavio's bracelet comes into view over Tavi's shoulder—the touch of his guardian angel— and he whispers into Tavi's ear: "Everything will be fine." Because it's time for Tavi to move on by himself. It was going to happen anyway, so why not now that he still has a few traces of his younger self left on his skin. Let's go to the D.R., Tavi. Let's lie down on the beach and let the airplane noise wash over us like a wave. Kiss me, Tavi.

But when the ambulance siren cries out, Tavi awakes from his reverie and realizes he inhabits the other side, where he's completely alone and without guidance. All he can do now is run out and chase the ambulance down the street, calling out, "Papa! Papa! Papa!" while the old Haitian woman, who leans on her comfortable pillow on the sill, shakes her head as she goes along for the ride.

Notes and Permissions

Contributors

Julia Alvarez emigrated to the United States from the Dominican Republic in 1960, fleeing the dictatorship of Rafael Leonidas Trujillo. She is the author of numerous novels, including *How the García Girls Lost Their Accent*, *In the Time of Butterflies*, and most recently, *Saving the World*. A versatile artist, Alvarez has written books for children and young adults, several collections of poetry, and a number of nonfiction works, including *Once Upon a Quinceañera: Coming of Age in the USA*. With her husband, Bill Eichner, Alvarez founded Alta Gracia, a sustainable farm in the Dominican Republic that produces organic coffee and also serves as a literacy center. She currently lives in Vermont, where she is a writer in residence at Middlebury College.

Susan Y. Chi is the founding editor of the *KGB Bar Lit Magazine*. Her stories have been published in *Small Spiral Notebook*, *BOMB*, *Jabberwock Review*, and *Promethean*. Her nonfiction work has appeared in the *NYFA Current*, *BOMBLOG*, *KGB Bar Lit Magazine*, and in the anthology *Not Quite What I Was Planning: Six-Word Memoirs*. She has received fellowships and grants from the Goodman Writing Fund, Vermont Studio Center, and Summer Literary Seminars: Saint Petersburg, Russia. Her scientific work has been published in *The Journal of Virology* and *The American Journal of Human Genetics*. Currently, Susan is a freelance copywriter and a graduate student in psychology at Brooklyn College.

Nicole Cooley grew up in New Orleans. In 2010, she published two books of poetry: *Breach* (LSU Press, April 2010), which focuses on Hurricane Katrina and its aftermath, and *Milk Dress*, co-winner of the Kinereth Gensler Award (Alice James Books, November 2010). She has published two other books of poems and a novel. Cooley has been awarded the Walt Whitman Award from the Academy of American Poets, a "Discovery"/*The*

Nation Award, and the Emily Dickinson Award from the Poetry Society of America. She directs the new MFA Program in Creative Writing and Literary Translation at Queens College-City University of New York.

Marcy Dermansky is the author of the novels *Bad Marie* and *Twins*. *Bad Marie* is a Barnes & Noble Discover Great New Writers selection. Her short fiction has been published in *McSweeney's, Alaska Quarterly Review, Mississippi Review,* and *Indiana Review*. She lives in Astoria with her husband, writer Jürgen Fauth, and their daughter Nina. Visit her Web site, marcydermansky.com, or follow her on Twitter at twitter.com/mdermansky.

Jill Eisenstadt is the author of two novels, *From Rockaway* and *Kiss Out* (Knopf) and the co-writer and co-producer of the feature film *The Limbo Room*. Shorter work has appeared or been anthologized in the *New York Times, New York* magazine, *Vogue, Elle, Queens Noir, Best Sex Writing 2008,* and *Best of the New York Times City Section,* among other places. Jill teaches writing at The New School in New York City.

Rigoberto González is the author of eight books, most recently of the young adult novel, *The Mariposa Club,* and a story collection, *Men Without Bliss*. The recipient of Guggenheim and NEA fellowships, winner of the American Book Award, and the Poetry Center Book Award, he writes a Latino book column for the *El Paso Times* of Texas. He is a contributing editor for *Poets & Writers Magazine,* on the Board of Directors of the National Book Critics Circle, and is Associate Professor of English at Rutgers—Newark, State University of New Jersey.

Ron Hogan helped create the literary Internet by launching Beatrice.com in 1995. He is the author of *The Stewardess Is Flying the Plane,* a visual tribute to '70s Hollywood, and *Getting Right With Tao,* a modern version of the Tao Te Ching. He was also a contributor to the *New York Times* bestseller *Not Quite What I Was Planning* and the critical anthology *Secrets of the Lost Symbol*.

Marc Landas is a writer and filmmaker based in New York. He is the author of *The Fallen: A True Story of American POWs and Japanese Wartime Atrocities* (John Wiley & Sons, 2004). He currently serves as an editor at London-based European Food and European Laboratory magazines as well as their Web site, Scientist Live. He has contributed to a variety of news sources ranging from Fox News to the *L.A. Times*. Landas received his BA in Biology from New York University and his MA in English Literature from Queens College CUNY. He is currently filming a documentary: *Conversations With the Living: Globalization and the HIV/AIDS crisis in Haiti*.

Robert Lasner is the author of the novel *For Fucks Sake*, which Neal Pollack called "The End of American Literature." He is also editor in chief of Ig Publishing, a Brooklyn-based independent press that publishes original literary fiction and political and cultural nonfiction. He was raised in Fresh Meadows, Queens, and though he doesn't go back too often, he will occasionally make the trip down the LIE just to get a plain with cream cheese from Bagel Oasis.

Victor LaValle is the author of the short story collection *Slapboxing with Jesus* and two novels, *The Ecstatic* and *Big Machine*. Among his awards and fellowships are a 2010 Guggenheim Fellowship, a Whiting Writers' Award, a United States Artists Ford Fellowship, and the key to Southeast Queens. He lives in New York City.

Jocelyn Lieu is the author of a 9/11 memoir, *What Isn't There: Inside a Season of Change* (Nation Books, 2007), and a collection of stories, *Potential Weapons* (Graywolf Press, 2004), published in France with the title *Discordances* (Éditions Phébus, 2007). Her work has appeared in *110 Stories: New York Writes After September 11*, *Charlie Chan Is Dead*, the *Asian Pacific American Review*, and the *Denver Quarterly*, among other anthologies and journals.

Molly McCloy has published work in *Nerve, Slate*, and *Swink*. She lives in Tucson and is working on a memoir. Visit her Web site: mollymccloy.com.

Arthur Nersesian was born and raised in New York City. His tenth book, *Mesopotamia*, has just been published by Akashic Books. All his readings and event are listed on his Web site at ArthurNersesian.com.

Buzz Poole has written about books, music, art, and culture for numerous publications, including the *Village Voice, The Believer, Print*, and *San Francisco Chronicle*. He is the author of *Madonna of the Toast* (Mark Batty Publisher, 2007), an examination of surprising iconography, which the *New Statesman* named one of 2007's Best Underground Books. He is also the author of the short story collection *I Like to Keep My Troubles on the Windy Side of Things* (Fractious Press, 2010). He lives in Jackson Heights, Queens.

Margo Rabb was born and raised in Sunnyside, Queens. She's the author of *Cures for Heartbreak*, and her new novel, *Mad, Mad Love*, will be published by Random House in 2012. Her short stories and essays have been published in the *New York Times*, the *Atlantic Monthly*, *Zoetrope: All Story*, *One Story*, *Seventeen*, *Mademoiselle*, and elsewhere, and have been broadcast on National Public Radio. She received first prizes in the *Atlantic Monthly*, *Zoetrope*, and *American Fiction* contests, and a PEN Syndicated Fiction Award. Visit her online at margorabb.com.

Irina Reyn is the author of *What Happened to Anna K.: A Novel* and the editor of the nonfiction anthology *Living on the Edge of the World: New Jersey Writers Take on the Garden State*. Her fiction and nonfiction have appeared in *San Francisco Chronicle*, *Los Angeles Times*, *Town & Country Travel*, *Poets & Writers*, *One Story*, *Tin House*, *LIT*, *Guernica*, *Five Chapters*, and other publications. She teaches creative writing at the University of Pittsburgh.

Roger Sedarat is Assistant Professor in the MFA Program in Creative Writing and Literary Translation at Queens College, CUNY. He is the author of two poetry collections: *Dear Regime: Letters to the Islamic Republic*, which won Ohio University Press's Hollis Summers' Prize, and *Ghazal Games* (forthcoming, Ohio University Press). He also has a forthcoming psychoanalytical study of landscape in New England poetry (Cambria). His translations and original poems have appeared in such journals as *New England Review*, *Atlanta Review*, and *Poet Lore*.

Margarita Shalina was born in Leningrad and raised on New York's Lower East Side. Her poetry has appeared in *3AM Magazine*, *At-Large Magazine*, *Poems for the Retired Nihilist V. 2* (Fortune Teller Press, UK), and *EvergreenReview.com*. She was a contributing translator to *Contemporary Russian Poetry* (Dalkey Archive Press). Her essays and reviews have been published in *PULSE/Berlin*, *ZEEK Magazine*, *ThreePercent.com*, and *The Poetry Project Newsletter*. She resided in Maspeth, Queens, for eight years.

Nicole Steinberg is an editor at large of *LIT* and her poetry has appeared in publications such as *No Tell Motel*, *BOMB*, *Gulf Coast*, *Barrow Street*, *Barrelhouse*, and *Coconut*. She is the author of the chapbook *Birds of*

Tokyo (Dancing Girl Press) and the curator and founder of Earshot, a Brooklyn-based reading series dedicated to emerging writers. She hails from all over Queens, New York, and currently lives in Philadelphia.

Mark Swartz is author of the novels *Instant Karma* and *H₂O*. He now lives with his wife and two daughters outside Washington, D.C. after five years in Forest Hills, Queens.

Jayanti Tamm received her MFA in Creative Writing at American University in Washington, D.C. Jayanti's works have been published in literary journals in the United States and Canada. In 2000, she was nominated for a Pushcart Prize. Her memoir, *Cartwheels in Sari: A Memoir of Growing Up Cult*, was published by Random House in 2009. Jayanti is an English Professor at Ocean County College where she teaches creative writing. Visit her at jayantitamm.com.

Juanita Torrence-Thompson was nominated as Woman of the Year 2009 by the American Biographical Institute Board for International Research. The American Association of University Women (AAUW) named her a Woman Who Makes a Difference & Is Dedicated to Diversity. Poems from her sixth book, *Breath-Life* (Scopcraeft Press, 2009) were nominated for a Pushcart Prize. She is editor in chief, publisher, and owner of twenty-eight-year-old international *Mobius, The Poetry Magazine*, which was "best pick" of 2007, 2008, and 2009 by Small Magazine Review. Her book, *New York and African Tapestries* (Fly by Night Press, 2007), was also named "best pick" by Small Press Review. She is a former Adjunct Professor at the College of New Rochelle (New Rochelle, NY) and teaches poetry workshops. She also produces poetry salons at Lewis H. Latimer House Museum in Queens and writes as a poetry columnist in Queens, NY and Massachusetts newspapers. She has read in the U.S., Canada, South Africa, Singapore, and Switzerland. Visit her online at poetrytown.com.

Marissa Walsh is the author of the comic memoir *Girl with Glasses: My Optic History* and the YA novel *A Field Guide to High School*; co-author of *Tipsy in Madras: A Complete Guide to '80s Preppy Drinking*; and editor of the YA anthologies *Not Like I'm Jealous or Anything: The Jealousy Book* and *Does This Book Make Me Look Fat?* A former children's book editor, she looks both ways before crossing Queens Boulevard.

John Weir is the author of two novels, *The Irreversible Decline of Eddie Socket* (HarperCollins, 1989) and *What I Did Wrong* (Viking, 2006). His fiction and nonfiction have appeared in various magazines, newspapers, and journals, including *Rolling Stone*, the *New York Times*, *Details*, *Spin*, *Tri-Quarterly*, and *Bloom*, and in several anthologies, including *Waves: An Anthology of New Gay Fiction* (Vintage, 1994), *Taking Liberties: Gay Men's Essays on Politics, Culture & Sex* (Richard Kasak Books, 1996), and *Between Men: Best New Gay Fiction* (Carroll & Graf, 2007). He is the Associate Chair of English at Queens College/CUNY, in Flushing, Queens, and a member of the Creative Writing faculty for their MFA program in Creative Writing and Translation.